When We Were the Kennedys

"In her intimate but expansive memoir, Monica Wood explores not only her family's grief but also the national end of innocence. Braiding her own story of mourning together with the heartbreak all around her, Wood has written a tender memoir of a very different time." — *O Magazine*

"This is an extraordinarily moving book, so carefully and artfully realized. . . . Monica Wood displays all her superb novelistic skills in this breathtaking, evocative new memoir. Wow." — **Ken Burns, filmmaker**

"It's a pleasure to linger with her elegant prose, keen eye, and grace of thought." — *Reader's Digest*

"A shining example of everything a memoir should be." — *U.S. Catholic Magazine*

"[A] terrific book, telling the story of Wood's family after the sudden death of her father when she was only nine. That's sad, of course, but the book isn't about being sad, it's about being a family. It's also about an era — the year was 1963 — and draws a parallel between Wood's story and the national loss of President Kennedy." — *Orion Magazine*

"Wood's gorgeously wrought new book . . . is a sharp, stunning portrait of a family's grief and healing, and it also offers a refreshing lens through which to view the JFK tragedy, as his family's loss helps the Woods feel less adrift in their own sea of anguish."   — *The Washingtonian*

"This year millions of words will be printed about the 50th anniversary of the assassination. . . . None will be as moving as *When We Were the Kennedys*. . . . Her brilliant, lyrical words pin us to Mexico . . . the time . . . those hopeful days before the 'mighty, mighty Oxford' went down under a cascade of labor disputes . . . before all the bright, ethereal promises of Camelot vanished."   — *Yankee Magazine*

"A gorgeous, gripping memoir. I don't know that I've ever pulled so hard for a family."
    — **Mike Paterniti, author of** *Driving Mr. Albert*

"The finest memoirs need not only a compelling story, but reflection and insight that transform the material so that the reader is moved and changed. Wood [uses] a novelist's skill to create thrilling moments of understanding."
    — *New Maine Times*

"Monica Wood is a stunning writer. . . . If I were standing beside you, I would press this book into your hands."
    — **Lily King, author of** *The Pleasing Hour*
    and *Father of the Rain*

"A lesson in family and communal ties, this book is a perfect summer read."   — *Bangor Daily News*

"A tender, plaintive . . . genuinely compelling depiction of family grief . . . a bittersweet, end-of-innocence family drama."   —*Kirkus*

"Wood's book . . . goes much beyond the story of her family's grief. The book is a meditation on time. . . . It's also a record of a vanished way of life . . . it avoids sentimentalizing small-town life. . . . By bringing such a town to life, with all its complexities and imperfections, it's to Monica Wood's great credit that she goes a long way to answering these questions."
                                    —*The New Yorker* online

"Readers of Monica Wood have long marveled at her powers of narrative conjuration, her ability to summon characters and landscapes and all-but-forgotten modes of living. . . . *When We Were the Kennedys*, a work of nonfiction, takes a very different approach: tipping present-day readers out of our armchairs and iPads and dropping us half a century into the past. . . . Most readers will feel a comparable surprise, I think, in discovering how easily they can lose themselves in a life story so unlike their own."   —*Down East Magazine*

"[Characters] all come alive through her evocative, colorful, gentle prose, the reader frequently left with either a tearful or a joyful heart. . . . *When We Were the Kennedys* is a powerfully written literary treasure that deserves many readers. It's the kind of book you will certainly want to read more than once."
                                    —*Catholic Sentinel*

When We Were
the Kennedys

A Memoir from Mexico, Maine

Christmas 2015

MONICA WOOD

*For Bob,
via your lovely daughter
Jean, with best wishes.*

Mariner Books
Houghton Mifflin Harcourt
BOSTON   NEW YORK

Warmly,

Monica Wood

First Mariner Books edition 2013
Copyright © 2012 by Monica Wood

For information about permission to reproduce selections from this book,
write to Permissions, Houghton Mifflin Harcourt Publishing Company,
215 Park Avenue South, New York, New York 10003.

www.hmhbooks.com

Library of Congress Cataloguing in Publication Data
Wood, Monica.
When we were the Kennedys : a memoir from Mexico, Maine / Monica Wood.
p. cm.
ISBN 978-0-547-63014-4   ISBN 978-0-544-00232-6 (pbk.)
1. Wood, Monica. 2. Authors, American — 20th century — Biography.
3. Mexico (Me. : Town) — Biography. I. Title.
PS3573.05948Z46 2012
813'.54 — dc22   [B]   2011016069

Book design by Brian Moore

Printed in the United States of America
DOC 10 9 8 7 6 5

Credit: Gregory Orr, "This is what was bequeathed us" from *How Beautiful the Beloved*.
Copyright © 2009 by Gregory Orr. Reprinted with the permission of Copper Canyon
Press, www.coppercanyonpress.org.

For Denise Vaillancourt, who shared her father

Author's Note

This is a memoir: the truth as I recall it. You will find herein no composite or invented characters, no rearranged chronologies, no alterations in the character or appearance of the people I remember. I changed only one name. One chapter contains a blizzard that my sisters now inform me occurred on a different occasion; and indeed, when I looked up weather for November 1963 I found not only no blizzard, but—astonishingly—no snow to speak of. The inaccurate memory is so embedded in my psyche, however, so inextricable from the remembered events of that chapter, that in the end I decided to leave it alone. Otherwise, events or processes I could not remember with accuracy or was too young at the time to understand—for example, papermaking, strike politics, the specific character of my father's work—I filled out as accurately as I could through research, the venerable *Rumford Falls Times*, and the memories of others. The bulk of this story, however, results from my having been an observant child living in a vibrant place and time.

This Is What Was Bequeathed Us

BY GREGORY ORR

This is what was bequeathed us:
This earth the beloved left
And, leaving,
Left to us.

No other world
But this one:
Willows and the river
And the factory
With its black smokestacks.

No other shore, only this bank
On which the living gather.

No meaning but what we find here.
No purpose but what we make.

That, and the beloved's clear instructions:

Turn me into song; sing me awake.

Contents

Prologue: My Mexico

I N MEXICO, MAINE, where I grew up, you couldn't find a single Mexican.

We'd been named by a band of settlers as a shout-out to the Mexican revolutionaries — a puzzling gesture, its meaning long gone — but by the time I came along, my hometown retained not a shred of solidarity, unless you counted a bottle of Tabasco sauce moldering in the door of somebody's fridge. We had a badly painted sombrero on the WELCOME TO MEXICO sign, but the only Spanish I ever heard came from a scratched 45 of Doris Day singing "Que Sera, Sera."

In fourth grade, after discovering that the world included a country called Mexico, I spent several befuzzled days wondering why it had named itself after us. Sister Ernestine adjusted my perspective with a pull-down map of the world, on which the country of Mexico showed up as a pepper-red presence and its puny namesake did not appear at all.

In high summer, when tourists in paneled station wagons caravanned through town on their way to someplace else, hankies pressed comically to their noses against the stench of paper being made, I sat with my friends on the stoop of Nery's Market to play License Plate. Sucking on blue Popsicles, we observed the procession of vehicles carrying strangers we'd never glimpse again, and accumulated points for every out-of-state plate. These people didn't linger to look around or buy anything, though once in a while a woman (always a woman, with the smiley red lips all women had then) popped out of an idling car to ask the posse of sunburnished children, *Why Mexico?*

We looked at one another. I was the one in the wrinkled T-shirt bought at the Alamo by my priest uncle, Father Bob, who loved to travel. Or maybe that was my little sister, Cathy, or my next-bigger sister, Betty, or one of our friends. Who could tell one kid from the next? White kids in similar clothes; Catholic children of millworkers and housewives. We lived in triple-decker apartment buildings — we called them "blocks" — or in nondescript houses that our fathers painted every few years. The only Mexico we knew was this one, ours, with its single main street and its one bowling alley and its convent and church steeples and our fathers over there, just across the river, toiling inside a brick-and-steel complex with heaven-high smokestacks that shot great, gorgeous steam clouds into the air so steadily we couldn't tell where mill left off and sky began.

Like most Irish Catholic families in 1963, mine had a boiled dinner on Sundays after Mass and salmon loaf on Fridays. We had pictures of Pope John and President John and the Sacred Heart of Jesus hung over our red couch, and on holidays my big brother, the frontman in a local band called the Impacts, came with his wife and babies and guitar to sing story songs packed with repentant jailbirds and useless regret and soldiers bleeding to death on heathery fields. In my friend Denise Vaillancourt's French Catholic family they ate meat pies— *"tourtières"*—on Christmas Eve and sang comic Québécois songs about mistaken identity and family kerfuffles. I had another friend, Sheila, who lived just our side of the Mexico-Rumford bridge, in a Protestant, two-child, flood-prone, single-family house; and another friend, Janet, who lived atop her parents' tavern, the regulars marshmallowed onto the barstools by three in the afternoon listening to Elvis on the jukebox. At St. Theresa's we greeted our teachers with a singsong *"Bonjooour, ma Soeur,"* diagrammed morally loaded sentences at flip-top desks, and drew flattering pictures of the Blessed Mother. We went to Mass on Sunday mornings and high holy days, singing four-part *Tantum Ergo*s from the choir loft in a teamwork reminiscent of our fathers sweating out their shifts in noisy, cavernous rooms. The nuns taught us that six went into twelve twice, that the Declaration of Independence was signed in 1776, that California exported avocados and Maine exported paper—tons and tons of paper, the kind our fathers made.

Though our elders in Mexico—who spoke French, or Italian, or Lithuanian, or English with a lilt—cherished their cultural differences, which were deep and mysterious and preserved in family lore, what bound us, the children, was bigger and stronger and far more alluring than the past. It was the future we shared, the promise of a long and bountiful life.

The unlikely source of that promise penetrated our town like a long and endless sigh: the Oxford Paper Company, that boiling hulk on the riverbank, the great equalizer that took our fathers from us every day and eight hours later gave them back, in an unceasing loop of shift work.

"The Oxford," we chummily called it, as if it were our friend. From nowhere in town could you not see it.

The mill. The rumbling, hard-breathing monster that made steam and noise and grit and stench and dreams and livelihoods—and paper. It possessed a scoured, industrial beauty as awesome and ever-changing as the leaf-plumped hills that surrounded us. It made a world unto itself, overbearing and irrefutable, claiming its ground along the Androscoggin, a wide and roiling river that cracked the floor of our valley like the lifeline on a palm. My father made his living there, and my friends' fathers, and my brother, and my friends' brothers, and my grandfather, and my friends' grandfathers. They crossed the footbridge over the river's tainted waters, carrying their lunch pails into the mill's overheated gullet five, six, sometimes seven days a week.

In every household in town, the story we children heard—between the lines, from mothers, fathers, mémères and pépères, nanas and nonnas, implied in the merest gesture of the merest day—was this: The mill called us here. To have you.

This was one powerful story. Powerful and engulfing, erasing all that came before, just like the mill that had made this story possible. In each beholden family, old languages were receding into a multicultural twilight as the new, sun-flooded story took hold: the story of us, American children of well-paid laborers, beneficiaries of a dream. Every day our mothers packed our fathers' lunch pails as we put on our school uniforms, every day a fresh chance on the dream path our parents had laid down for us. Our story, like the mill, hummed in the background of our every hour, a tale of quest and hope that resonated similarly in all the songs in all the blocks and houses, in the headlong shouts of all the children at play, in the murmur of all the graces said at all the kitchen tables. In my family, in every family, that story—with its implied happy ending—hinged on a single, beautiful, unbreakable, immutable fact: Dad.

Then he died.

When We Were the Kennedys

1

Morning

THE MORNING OF my father's death begins like all
other mornings: my mother stirring oatmeal at the
stove, cats twining around her legs, parakeet jab-
bering on her shoulder. My oldest sister, Anne, who teaches
English at the high school, is at work already; and Dad,
who got up at five-thirty for first shift, is putting a crew together in the spongy air of the Oxford's woodyard. Or so
we believe. Betty and Cathy and I, our hair starched from
sleep, rouse ourselves after Mum's second call. We attend St.
Theresa's, a French Catholic elementary school that we can
see, over the rooftop of my friend Denise's block on Brown
Street, from our third-floor kitchen window. I'm in fourth
grade, Cathy in second. Betty—mentally disabled (we say
"retarded" back then)—is also in second grade, for the third
time; she sits at the desk next to Cathy, who lately has been
teaching her to knit, a suggestion from Sister Edgar, who
has just about run out of ideas.

Below us, on the second floor, come the muted morning sounds from the Hickeys: That's Norma leaving for work as a secretary at the power company. Her mother, the only one-armed person I know, scoops up the *Lewiston Daily Sun* and snaps it open in a nimble abracadabra, one of her most enthralling sleight-of-one-hand feats. Mr. Hickey—a sweet, frail man "let go" from the mill for his ailing eyes and lungs—stays inside, drinking tea from Mrs. Hickey's scalloped cups.

Below that, on the first floor, our Lithuanian landlady begins her daily cooking of cabbage and other root vegetables that smell more or less like the mill. The ancient Norkuses speak halting English, charge us seven dollars a week in rent, and engage in an intermittent skirmish with Mum over whether we kids should be allowed to bring our friends up to visit. *Too much stairs*, they say, which could mean almost anything.

In the Norkus block, where we live, the three apartments are identically laid out—four rooms, a screened porch in front, an open porch landing in back—but each has a separate, and separately revelatory, air of foreignness. The Norkus apartment, densely furnished, emanates a steamy, over-draped blurriness that I still associate with all Lithuanian households. The Hickeys' floor, quiet and tidy, seems like a trick, its scrubbed interior latitudes magically expanded. Every time I enter, I think of the Popeye cartoon in which Olive Oyl peers into a tiny tent and finds the inside of the Taj Mahal. Our top floor, full of girls and mateless socks and hair doodads and schoolbooks and cats and unlaced Keds and molted feathers, operates on the same principle, in reverse: When you open our door, the physical world shrinks.

In this filled-to-brimming place on the morning of Dad's death, Mum's parakeet flutters down from her shoulder to perch on my oatmeal bowl, his scaly feet gripping the rim. He pecks at my breakfast, spattering gruel, gibbering words gleaned from my mother's patient repetitions. He can also sing and dance, but not now; Mum wants us at school on time and so far it doesn't look promising. Cathy appears, wearing half of her school uniform—the starched white blouse—and a slip. I'm half-dressed, too, in opposite: army-green skirt and pajama top. Mum presses our clothes in stages, so that is how we put them on. Outside, the morning radiates the particular cool of April. Betty comes last to eat, in full uniform, everything tucked and smoothed and buttoned up right, her ankle socks neatly creased. Mum always makes sure she's fully shipshape before moving on to us. We dawdle over orange juice as Cathy, against orders, puts the parakeet on a pencil to see if he'll do a spin; it's his best trick and kills the room every time. This is how mornings go, a tango of getting ready, each girl a separate challenge, Mum alternately shooshing us and making us *sit! sit! sit!* to eat.

I'm the slow eater. The "absent-minded" one. I watch out the window, but nothing looks different. Dad is already dead but I don't know this yet, can't imagine this. No shiver in the air catches my eye, no subtle darkening in the same old steam clouds cluttering the morning sky. I am nine years old; when I look out the window, all I see is Mexico—my Mexico, the only one that counts.

From here I see the Dohertys' back line hung with clothes. Next to them, the Gagnons'; we play with their girls and have a crush on Mrs. Gagnon, with her ripple of auburn hair. Catty-cornered from the Gagnons are the O'Neills, and then the Yarnishes, their driveway patrolled by a disgruntled crow that hollers, "Hiii Joe, hiii Joe!" all day long. The rest of the neighborhood fills out with Gallants and Fourniers and Burgesses and Nailises and Fergolas, a census that repeats to the town line of our stewpot town and crosses the river to Rumford, the mill's official home.

We get chocolate cake whenever we want—Mum's splendid recipe survives to this day. Lemon tea bread, cherry pie, yeast doughnuts, just ask! We have a talking bird and priest uncle. We never have to clean our plates or finish our milk. Dad comes home every day with candy in his pockets. Father Bob, Mum's baby brother, comes to town once a week and sometimes says the First Friday Mass, where all our friends simmer with envy that God's young, dashing stand-in belongs to us. Mum gives us *dollars* to bring to school to save the pagan babies. Last year Dad bought a 1962 sea-green Chrysler Newport, brand-new. We think we're rich.

We *are* rich.

Dad, like most people, must have applied a kind of rhythm to his workday. I followed that rhythm in my mind many times after that morning: his feet hitting the floor upon waking, the morning ablutions, the soft exchanges with my mother as she hands him his lunch pail and clears his breakfast plate, the door clicking shut behind him, the three downward flights. Possibly he stops to pet the Norkuses' cat, Tootsie (like all men in our family, Dad is a cat man), before stepping into the street.

Perhaps he is in pain; I hope not. Even so, his last mortal moments are swaddled by the familiar. He leaves us, turns right onto Gleason Street, passes the O'Neills', the Gagnons', the Velushes', turns right again at Miss Caliendo's onto Mexico Avenue to the Venskus block, where they rent out their row of six attached garages at the back of the wide, blacktopped driveway, each bay just wide enough to fit one car.

Perhaps he stops here for a moment, gazing down that

long paved drive, for at times he still deeply misses the furrowed fields and quilted hills of Prince Edward Island, Canada, and the siblings who remain on the family farm. Is this crisp April morning one of those times? It's cold but the air contains the coming spring. So, yes, he stops—right here, at the head of the driveway, hanging on to the post—to take it in. He doesn't yet know he's running out of breath; he thinks it's memory doing this, the memory of the long dirt lane to the homestead he left at age twenty. The farmhouse with its blistered roof. The pumped water. The lilacs and hollyhocks. The neighborhood of colorful characters who live along the road.

It must be memory doing this, squeezing his chest, summoning an anointed place that could not give him what he found here: steady, decent, good-paying work. He found his wife here, had five children over twenty years. His youngest, Cathy, is eight; his oldest, a son who lives ten miles away, will turn twenty-seven in a week. Is he thinking of us now? He lets go of the post, steps onto the blacktop, walks—slow, so slow—to the garage door, intending with all his heart to put in another blessed day of a life he never dreamed possible.

In another eight years he can retire, this man who has never taken a vacation or owned a house. Does he think of this as he reaches for the handle? Can he picture long visits back to the Island, then endless, easeful days back here, tilling the borrowed plot he keeps in his father-in-law's yard just a few houses up the street from where he stands now—tight-chested, filling with memory—at six o'clock in the morning, April 25, 1963, in the first waking of an ordinary day? *Here we go*, people say at these humdrum moments of repetition, the day's momentum released by the turn of a key or the punch of a time card or, in Dad's case, the sliding open of a garage door. The door makes a loud, sacrilegious *clang* against the morning quiet.

Here—.

A bursting in his chest.

He drops his lunch pail. Sees a flash of light. Thinks of us in our innocent beds.

And he's gone.

I hope he had a moment of purity, a clearing of all thought and memory, a beautiful surrender. Dad was a Catholic who believed in the saints. I hope he saw the face of God.

The teenage boy who found Dad grew up to be a stage singer of no small reputation. But on this morning he's just a neighborhood kid, an older boy whose mother teaches piano. He's home from college and on his way to Fisher's Store, where he works sometimes as a clerk. Passing the Venskus block, humming an aria he's been rehearsing with his teachers, he makes a disbelieving double take.

Is that—?

The sight of my father lying in front of the garage door, cap knocked off his head, lunch pail spilled at his feet, must surely endure in his memory. He thuds down the blacktop, hard and quick on his feet, but Dad has flown, he is no longer a person, and the boy can see this. He runs to the back doors of the Venskus block, pounds on a window, a door, until people come running, but the commotion stays tucked inside them, nobody speaks above a whisper. A man they know is lying here dead, his family just over there; if you crane your neck and look up, over the roof of these garages, you can see the skeletal back stairs of the Norkus block, where inside, on the third floor, this man's widow, who does not yet know she's a widow, is pouring oatmeal into a pot of water, humming something pleasant and known.

Somebody calls the constable. The boy with the marvelous voice says a prayer.

I have met this now-grown-up boy a handful of times over the years. I have watched him perform. He sings in a rich, operatic tenor, heart-crushingly beautiful, in which, I believe, Dad's final moments still live.

We were an ordinary family; a mill family, not the stuff of opera. And yet, beginning with the singing boy who found Dad, my memory of that day reverberates down the decades as something close to music. Emotion, sensation, intuition. I see the day—or chips and bits, as if looking through a kaleidoscope—but I also hear it, a faraway composition in the melodious language of grief, a harmonized affair punctuated now and again by an odd, crystalline note fluting up on its own. A knock on a door. A throaty cry.

Not long after the boy pounds on the Venskuses' windows, Mr. Cray, our town constable, comes plodding up the driveway of the Norkus block like a horse in mud. Mr. Cray, florid and hefty like Dad, moving with Dad's heavy step, the first dissonant note of the day. I squint down three stories as I dawdle over my oatmeal. "Mum, Mr. Cray is here."

My mother bursts into song. Or so it seems, on this morning in which nothing is as it seems.

Ohhh, my mother sings. *Ohhh.*

For a moment—before the first stir of alarm, that tight knot of suspicion struggling up to my throat—I assume that Mum's keening will be shortly explained, will become another glinting droplet in the blizzard of information that composes any childhood. Her hands fly to her forehead, she whirls around to face the door, egress blocked by a laundry basket and ironing board that she bulls her way around.

7

We're confused now, and getting scared. What is Mum doing? As we listen to Mr. Cray's footfalls on the stairs—a sound exactly like Dad coming home from work—the morning acquires a pitiless momentum. Mr. Cray passes the Norkuses' on the first floor, keeps going; passes the Hickeys' on the second floor, keeps going; and finally stops outside our door, which my mother flings open, crying out, "He's dead, isn't he!"

Who? Who does she mean? Big Mr. Cray, as formless and crumpled-looking as a pile of warm sheets, appears in our shoe-filled front hall. A strange commotion arises there. I begin walking backwards, something we do sometimes for fun. Backwards, retreating from the noise in my mother's throat, backwards into our bedroom, backwards, trying to reverse time. Betty waits there, sitting on her bunk, alarmed but uncomprehending, her eyes pale as dimes. Cathy—the bravest, the one who takes nothing at face value—stands her ground in the kitchen, where the morning will take on the shellac of permanence and become the museum piece we will all come back to again and again, seeing something new each time in this preserved, precious thing.

At last, Cathy barrels into our room, crying, "Dad died!" She's eight years old, the announcer, the town crier, the loud one. And she's blubbering loudly now, drowning out the disquieting sound just outside our door. Her army-green sash divides the white of her blouse but her skirt still hasn't made it from the ironing board. She's got a hairbrush stuck in her hair. "Daddy's dead!" she announces again, making it true, understanding it all of a piece, accepting a sorrow she will never quite get over. I cry, too—instantly, violently—but my reaction feels less like grief (though how can I tell, having known none until now?) and more like the moment after a physical blow, that helpless empty space between the blow and the pain. Betty looks at us for a long moment, receiving the news more slowly, her eyes refusing to register the thing we say to her again and again, whispering first, then louder. Then louder. Until she cries.

Now we all know.

My mother will explain to us later that she dreamed it—three nights running, she dreamed that our fifty-seven-year-old father dropped dead on his way to work. She will wonder aloud whether she offered Mr. Cray any relief when she met him at the door already speaking the words he dreaded to utter. All that was left for him was to say yes.

Anne gets the news at the high school, where she's fully entered a cool spring morning in that alternative, all-consuming world. Hello to her carrel-mates in the English/History office. Coffee in the black-and-orange Mexico Pintos mug. A commotion of students in the lobby down the hall, a faraway sound like muffled applause. A copy of the *Lewiston Daily Sun* lies on a table littered with stained spoons and spent sugar packets. She glances at the headlines. Yesterday an integrationist was killed in Alabama, and now President Kennedy has sent his brother Bobby to talk to the governor. Across the globe, a country called Laos simmers into civil war; this, too, concerns the president. All this seems so far away, but she often twines current events into her examination of literature, just as Father Bob, known for his stirring, everyman preaching, twines Walter Cronkite into his Sunday sermons. She shakes a stubborn fountain pen, going over notes for her first-period English class, adjusts her hem before stepping into the waxy corridor.

She must be so happy.

Her teaching career will prove long and fruitful, but today, in the dwindling of year one, she is probably too young, too in love with literature, to see the folly of teaching Spenser's *The Faerie Queene* to a galootish group of "shop boys." They must love looking at her, this cute ninety-pounder in a lavender skirt and vest, the white ruffles of her blouse leaving ripples of motion like angel feathers as she smarts down the hall in her French heels. Her hair is pulled into a chignon; she wears gold clip-on earrings and a glimmersome bracelet, onyx disks trimmed in gold, a present from Father Bob, who loves buying jewelry for his girls.

My sister loves clothes—"maybe too much," she once confessed to Father Bob, who reminded her that as a young man St. Francis of Assisi was himself quite the snappy dresser. And anyway, fashion provides the underpinnings of her teaching philosophy, the bones in the corset: Students are worth dressing up for. When you enter a classroom, any day, every day, you should look as if you plan to accept an award.

At first bell, the boys storm the room in a great collapse of size-twelve shoes and day-old stubble, smelling of machine oil and Brylcreem. They look older than their teacher (one of them probably is), but my sister—though pretty and fragile-looking and dressed for spring and still living at home and twenty-two years old and not yet possessed of a driver's license—carries an air of grit that she will shortly put to use in a way she cannot, in this hopeful, entering moment, foresee.

"We didn't get it," the boys tell her about their homework, sixteen lines of Spenser.

"Did you read it?" Her lipstick today is a shade called Peachstone.

"Of course we read it!"

"Did you think about it?"

"Uh—"

"Exactly. It's not enough to read. You have to think. So. Let's think."

As they think, someone—perhaps Mr. Cray—leaves a knotted message with the school secretary, a message further tangled by whoever delivers it to Anne. A student, most likely, one of the good girls who work in the office during study hall. This girl ferries the message through war-era corridors to the windowed, oaken door of my sister's classroom. There has been a mishap in Miss Wood's household but nobody seems to know quite what.

Anne experiences a lurch of fear for her little sisters, then looks back at her boys, who are struggling over Edmund Spenser's lapidary raptures: *Mirrour of grace and majestie divine . . . shed thy faire beames into my feeble eyne.* Whatever appears in their teacher's *eyne* at this moment makes them go silent as snow.

"Excuse me," she tells them. "I've been—summoned." The nuns at her college used words like this. Composing herself, she lingers a moment at the too-big wooden lectern, her hands grasping its cumbersome sides. She smoothes the pages of the open anthology, the teacher's edition, too wide and too heavy and hard-backed. Everything in this room is bigger than she is. "Duane," she says. Her throat is all dried up. "And Ed. You're in charge." Two lunky boys in short sleeves stand up, nearly step on each other getting to the front of the room, where they will lead the class in the cracking open of sixteenth-century lyrics. They're good with a hammer and she trusts them to do it right.

She leaves the room at a normal clip, closes the door behind her, then begins to run, her toes jamming into her pointy shoes, down the long corridor to the office, where the school secretary offers her the phone.

"Come home," Mum says. "I need you." She does not say why and Anne does not ask.

Scarcely one downhill mile separates the high school from our block. The principal gives Anne a ride, offers to come upstairs. "No," she tells him, trembling now with alarm. "I'm sure it's fine."

Then we hear her, coming back to us, quick-quick, her patent-leather pumps puncturing each wooden tread—first floor, second floor, third floor, quickening as she nears us, quick through the door.

The clamor stuns her but in she comes. Crying baby sisters. Mother heart-shocked in a chair. Ironing board still heaped with unpressed laundry, a bottle of starch dripping over a soggy blouse. The parakeet dancing on his perch, *sugartime sugartime sugartime* he sings, nervously back-and-forthing on his spongy feet, he wants out, he wants out, he wants out. The cats have fled to hide inside things inside other things. The shape of our family has been upended and rearranged, its roof flattened, its gateposts ripped from the earth by God's own brutal hand, and only the animals know enough to make a run for it.

Stepping into this exploded, delicate thing that will forever now be us, Anne decodes the muddled message at last. So simple, so razoringly precise: Dad died.

She pulls herself together and, in the lingo of our time and place, begins to "do" for us. Make the calls. Greet the visitors. Feed tea and toast to our weeping mother. Fold up the ironing board. Finish the dishes.

Someone has to "do." And so. She does.

My brother, a married Air Force veteran with two boys, is a pipefitter in the mill, where he gets the news in a similarly convoluted way. "You're wanted at home," somebody says. So Barry drives heart-thumpingly home—to *his* home, a little house in Dixfield, the next town downriver.

"What's wrong?" he asks Nila, who's buttoning Stevie into a little shirt after walking Mike to his kindergarten.

His wife looks up, alarmed. "Nothing. What are you doing here?"

"You didn't call for me?"

She shakes her head, eyes darkening. "No. Someone called for you?"

So Barry calls the mill back, confused. "You must have another John Wood," he tells the front office. In paperwork he goes by "John"—John Barry. Anne is Mary Anne; on Prince Edward Island you call children by their hidden names. In this year of 1963, the mill at its booming peak, there might well be another John Wood somewhere among three thousand employees scattered over three shifts, someone from Byron or Roxbury or West Peru or any one of our surrounding towns, another John Wood wanted at home for a reason nobody has the nerve to explain.

"Are you John?"

"Yes."

"You work in the pipers?"

"Yes."

"Your father died this morning."

He sprints back to his car, drives too fast to Mexico, and thunders up those three flights.

We do not see my brother often, but when we do, he brings his wife and boys and his beloved May Belle acoustic guitar and takes over the parlor, where we beg for melodramatic rockabilly songs about heartbreak and missed chances in a velvety timbre that Dad called "fearful-grand singing."

But he brings nothing with him today but a powerful sense of dread as he bursts through the door and looks into the drained face of our mother and asks, "Is it true?"

Our apartment harbors few places to grieve in private: four rooms and only two with a door. Barry drags a chair from the kitchen and slips into the bedroom, where after a few minutes I crack the door open to the astonishing sight of my adult brother, facing away from me, sitting astride the spindly chair, his head down, his arms cradling the chair back, a pose not unlike the one he sometimes takes with his guitar. His shoulders heaving up and down, he forms soft, strangulated notes that stir me much the way those lyrics about heart-broke lovers often do. I've never seen him, or any man, cry. For a brief, melting moment I believe I'm hearing the sound of my brother singing.

Before Anne came home—thirty stopped minutes, a grotesque, ongoing *now* in which our mother shed her former self like a wind-shook tree—we children aged with fear. Our mother was both overly present—all that gasping and keening—and also eerily far away. We stood at the edge of the kitchen, knotted together, edging first toward and then away from those awful sounds, but because we, too, were yowling and keening there was nowhere safe. "I've lost my best friend," Mum cried, to no one, to God, to the ceiling. "I've lost my best friend." When she hid her face in her hands we mobbed her, petting her hair, her arms, then backed away again as her up-gushing grief took another vocal turn.

"What do we do?" Cathy whispered. She was standing so close that the heat of her breath moistened my neck. She and Betty looked at me; I was the one in fourth grade.

"I don't know," I whispered back. "I don't know I don't know."

More hot breath on my neck. "You have to get Anne."

But how would I get the number? And who would answer? And how would I tell them what was happening, Mum bent at the waist, Mr. Cray thumping back down the stairs, everybody crying? But then the phone rang and Mum said, *Come home, I need you*, and for a second I thought, *That's Dad on the other end, maybe that's Dad on the other end*, until Mum squeezed me too hard—my arm hurting, my hand twisted between her body and mine—and then let go because she couldn't stand up, she had to sit, and then those terrifying, animal sounds gushed out again, and it seemed as if we were all stuck fast, stuck in one eternal moment, a locked trap of disbelief.

But now, a miracle, Anne is home—Anne's home!—and that encased moment geysers open, briefly cleansing our monstrous pain.

The door opens and opens. The phone rings and rings. People arrive and arrive and the day moves despite all, and we children, who had felt the queasy stirrings of duty—*At least you have your children*, Mr. Cray said—see now that nothing will be asked of us. We don't have to save Mum after all. We don't have to think up a way—think! think!—to call Dad back from heaven.

Childhood is over, but Anne's home, so we can still be children.

The rest of that morning, after Dad's unthinkable departure, fills with arrival. Father Bob, who will oversee Dad's funeral, comes home to us from his parish in Westbrook. He embraces Mum, blesses her—*In nomine Patris . . .*—murmurs into her neck another prayer or incantation or perhaps something only a baby brother can say to his fourteen-years-older sister, something in plain English. Whatever it is, it doesn't work; my mother sits again, vacant, wordless, her lips gently parted.

A priest in the room is supposed to smooth things over, heal confusion, make ritual out of chaos. I cling to my shaking uncle, to the familiar scent of his blacks — his rabat and collar and jacket — but there are so many people here now, another neighbor coming through the door, and here are Aunt Rose and Cumpy — my aunt and my grandfather — and two of Dad's workmates from the mill, and after a while I realize that Father Bob, too, has headed for the bedroom — Barry has gone back home to break the news — where he lies on the bed with his black shoes on. I steal over to my own bedside, terrified.

Men crying everywhere.

He stares at the ceiling. Glasses fogged, cheeks gone scarlet, mouth quavering so badly it seems poised to slide off his face. He does not look at me but knows I'm here. "Is it all right for a man to cry, Monnie?" he asks me. He loved Dad more than he loves his own father.

What kind of question is this? What kind of question is this? I answer with another question: "Yes?"

"That's right," he says, though I can barely hear him. "It's all right for a man to cry."

I don't know what to do with this information; I'm afraid to touch him, my beloved uncle who has loved me in turn for as long as I can remember. He makes painful, held-in, small-animal sounds, his tears pooling on the pillows I share with Cathy. Then someone — I think it's Anne — touches my shoulder, releases me from this too-private moment, and leads me back out to the kitchen, now filled with people, tears all over.

Mrs. Hickey shows up with a tuna pie; the O'Neills drop off some biscuits; other neighbors, too many to sort, bring meat loaf, deviled eggs, soda bread. At some point, some-where between Mr. Cray's visit and Father Bob's arrival, somebody asks, "Where's Cathy?"

Everyone looks at me.

"I don't know."

I don't. Their faces scare me. The whole house has tilted somehow, and it's hard to see, and to hear, and everybody seems to be saying something to somebody who is saying something to somebody else. Those first few hours are like being caught inside a washing machine, an agitated drown-ing.

"What do you mean, you don't *know*?" Mum says, panick-ing, alive again after a zombielike lull that I have no way of recognizing as shock. My mother, who never panics over anything, starts to shake. "People don't just vanish into thin air."

But Dad did. His soul, anyway. His baptized soul lifted from his body and vanished into thin air.

On any other day, a vanishing child would present no ca-lamity. Kids always turn up, like cats, playing in a neigh-bor's yard or eating in some other kid's kitchen. Why does it matter that Cathy's gone missing? We're always missing. We live in an era when mothers throw their children into a teeming neighborhood with the instructions "I don't want to see you kids till supper."

But Mum is up now, her eyes darting. "Mother of Mary," she murmurs. All the adults are, suddenly, up.

Anne puts on a sweater, heads for the door. Where is Cathy?

"SHE WENT TO SCHOOL," says Betty, who speaks in stammering capital letters, and just then Cathy materializes from the thin air into which she vanished, having been sent back home from St. Theresa's, where she'd showed up in

Sister Edgar's second-grade classroom, her hair unbrushed but uniform complete, to slip behind her flip-top desk and take out her pencil and prepare to do Religion, which was the first subject of the day no matter what grade you were in.

"Why are you late?" Sister Edgar asked.

"My father died."

"When?"

My sister's pink quivering lip: "Now."

Sister Edgar, a young, kindly nun, stork-tall with dolorous dark eyes and long, lithe fingers, ushered Cathy back into the hall, assured her that her mother would surely prefer to have her near, then sent her home — one block away — with her unspent lunch money fisted into one hand.

"You went to school?" Mum says, incredulous, sitting down again with the weight of this fresh news. Her youngest child went to school, alone, carrying the unspeakable burden of Dad's death. Mum is raising good girls and this is what good girls do. Dad's bold-hearted girl, his favorite, has transformed herself within an hour into a child so invisible she can vanish into thin air and nobody, not even her own mother, will notice.

Something about Cathy's instinctive act of normalcy makes the thing that is happening newly unbearable. I go to the place where I, too, can disappear. I slink to a corner — a shadow of space between the couch and the door to the screen porch, with a book, or a sheaf of Dad's paper, and I bend my head to another family with a different story, either writing one or reading one. I stay there until Anne finds me and leads me back to the kitchen, which has filled with people and a flocklike physical warmth that brings an aimless, muffling comfort. We take turns nuzzling against our glassy-eyed mother, though nothing we do can cure what ails her.

Just before nightfall, when we can barely close the fridge for all the casseroles and have literally run out of places to sit, a final visitor arrives: a well-dressed stranger in a tie, his hair damp and neatly combed, his face grave with sympathy. Mum is sitting in the kitchen, same chair into which she collapsed hours ago after Mr. Cray said his yes. A silver pin glints from the stranger's brushed lapel: *Oxford Paper Company*.

This man, who looks like Don Ameche, Dad's favorite actor, is the mill manager. In memory he is tall, broad, solemn. My mother, who has not risen from her chair all day, rises for him.

"I'm so sorry," he says. His shoulders too wide, his jacket heavily structured. I've never seen a man in a suit like this.

Mum puts out her hands, which look thin and fairylike, and he folds them into his: large, pinkish, full of a confusing authority.

"I'm so sorry," he says again. "We're all so sorry."

How has Mum become so small? I look down; she's wearing the shoes she had on this morning: low, sensible heels, but pretty, with a strap. This is her full height, I can see, but it's different from the full height she woke up with.

"You didn't have to come," she tells the man, and now I hear an oddly vibrant note in her voice, an incongruous little trill that pierces the fog of this awful day, that softens the shock of her changed height. She is both larger, and smaller, than her real self as she keeps her hands in the hands of this man.

"We're praying for you," says the man. "For all of you."

"Thank you," my mother whispers. "It means so much to us that you came."

He stays only a few more moments—charged, bright, layered moments in which I feel both enthralled and muddled, honored and ashamed. An important man has come to see my mother; he resembles an actor; his condolences tip a scale that I did not know existed. His visit elevates Dad's standing; this much is clear. Which means this man is more important than Dad.

And that Dad cannot be, as I so long believed, the most important man in the world.

These intuitions provide my first, feeble inklings about social class and its myriad contradictions, its necessity in times of trauma, its cool, dispassionate lessons about who we are and where we are in the world.

It seems the whole town has come to see my family today, to offer food and sympathy and reassurance. Why do I not feel reassured? Instead, I experience a profound dislocation, a feeling like slipping on the shifting surface of my allotted scrap of God's earth, in the country of America, in the state of Maine, in the town of Mexico, my Mexico, the one Dad no longer lives in.

This morning we woke up as the Wood family. Who are we now?

2

Wake

SELECT CASKET. CALL relatives. Pay mortician. Get Mum through funeral. Anne, Anne, Anne, Anne. Did she choose Dad's clothes after tucking us in, picking through the closet with Mum, hunting up a Dad shirt that wasn't plaid, Dad pants that weren't work-green, Dad shoes that weren't boots with steel toes? *Plink, plink, plink* go the flimsy wire hangers, so quick they make sparks in the dark, fleeting past like a brief, bright life, releasing the scent of wood pulp and Camels. I see the clothes coming off the hangers, my sister's pink-lacquered fingernails working the buttonholes, Mum staring at the empty sleeves.

Anne must have done these things quick and birdlike, and yet when I peer back into the diorama of our stricken kitchen where the news breaks over and over, where three wailing girls set upon their big sister in a tide swell of misery and need, Anne appears to me in stillness. Poised in front of our round-shouldered fridge as if waiting for a camera click, somewhere at the middle of the morning, wholly still, her slender arms enfolding Betty, who leans against her as one might lean against a leafy tree. Like that tree, Anne is the thing that holds fast to the shifting ground.

Mexico has no funeral home but Rumford has two, Thibeault's and Meader's: one Catholic, one Protestant. While the adults go to Thibeault's to guard Dad's body, we girls have to stay with my friend Margie, who lives just behind us, one lot over. The Lavorgna block has a long front porch and barnlike garage. Anne walks us over there on the afternoon of our second day with no father, where we'll be supervised until after the evening calling hours.

"I'll be back for you after eight," she says.

"WHAT TIME IS EIGHT?" Loud is Betty's default setting; she never raises her voice from there.

"After *Superman* is over," Anne says.

"Do you dress up for a wake?" asks Cathy. All morning she had begged to go. Begged and begged.

"Yes."

"Is it like church?"

"A little bit. We'll say the rosary."

"Does everybody know about Dad?" I ask.

"Not everybody. A lot of people, though."

"What if somebody asks about Dad?"

Here is what Anne figures out, that already I'm living in dread of explaining the thing I have no word for. I can't bring myself to say the word *dead*. So she gives me a new word, my first writer's word.

"You say, 'deceased,'" she tells me. My big sister, my own future English teacher, instructing me already: "You say, 'deceased.'"

Mrs. Lavorgna opens the door, big friendly smile. A tall,

handsome woman, a chatty store clerk who drives her own car. "Hello, girls," she says. "We've been waiting for you."

"My father is deceased," I tell her.

"Oh, honey," she says. "I know."

I've been here many times to play with Margie, but this feels different. It's wrong and sad for the three of us to be here together, like storybook orphans at a stranger's door. Anne squeezes us each in turn. "You'll have fun."

We inch into the kitchen. Mrs. Lavorgna and Mum shared a room in the Rumford maternity ward when Margie and I were born, two women having midlife babies, and their passing resemblance—steel-gray hair and cat's-eye glasses—bestows an unexpected comfort now. As for Mr. Lavorgna (the butcher at Fisher's, where until yesterday Dad had stopped every night on his way home from work), as he stirs his bubbling spaghetti sauce in the steamy kitchen, we turn him into a faint shadow of Dad, despite his Italian good looks, his black hair and thin, tweezy mustache.

I'm used to this house. Last fall I'd skulked at the door of the Lavorgna garage, where a luckless deer hung by its antlered head, pink tongue gone gray and lolling, a tableau repeated all over town. *Dead*, I thought, staring into its un-lighted eyes. That Margie's jokey, kindly father—that any of Mexico's fathers—could have killed an animal so gentle-eyed, so soft-colored, stirred my insides with mystery. Dad had never killed anything, had been polite to ants and lady-bugs; and, because he'd been too young for the War to End All Wars and too old for the one after that, he had never, as far as I knew, touched a gun. Mum, for her part, had a super-stition about harming spiders, so we had to catch them in a Kleenex, put them in a cup, and escort them outdoors. My family didn't like dead things. I'd wanted so badly to touch

Mr. Lavorgna's deer, for I'd been reading about saints and their miracles. Did I have the touch? Could I raise the dead? In the end I kept my possible power to myself, fearful that it wouldn't work, or maybe that it would. Death—even of a deer—was God's business, and you were supposed to leave God's business alone.

In her customary chair just inside the kitchen door sits Margie's aged Lithuanian nana. Impossible to know what she thinks of the Wood children spending the evening of their father's wake in her household, for her English is impenetrable and she's not the type to converse with children anyway. I recall her as a lone figure, in her striped skirts and babushka, a throwback peasant lady plunked into the middle of 1960s America, condemned to die in an alien culture, gentling her carrots from their foreign soil as if they were a loved one's tender bones.

"Would you girls like something to eat?" Margie's father asks.

We glance at each other. "No, thank you." We haven't been schooled on rules regarding visiting orphans.

"*Ash-ash, ticka-ticka, push-push,*" Nana says, or something like it.

Margie saves us: "You wanna play in my room?"

Margie has Barbie *and* Ken *and* Midge *and* Skipper. She even has her own record player but only one record, "Orange-Colored Sky," a threadbare Doris Day song from the fifties that we listen to over and over, taking turns lip-synching and high-stepping while carrying Margie's mother's umbrella.

"My turn," Cathy says, grabbing the umbrella and twirling it as she dances, a trick Margie and I haven't thought of. "*I was dancing alonnng, thinking in sunshiiiine,*" she sings out loud, muffing the lyrics. Betty, our audience, appears rapt, making things worse. Cathy is pretending to be the real Doris Day, I believe, in order to get as far from me—and Betty, and the reason for our being here in Margie's room—as she can get. Her chopped hair jounces as she mugs and twirls and belts out the tune on a slight backbeat, sounding nothing at all like Doris Day, which in this strange long moment, thirty-seven hours after Dad's death, breaks my heart. Her umbrella work kills us, though: She hip-checks across the room in her bare feet and pedal pushers, rocking her shoulders, the umbrella swiveling like a live partner, so convincing in this memory that I can almost see the shadow person helplessly swinging along, there but not there, like the child version of herself that she's already leaving behind.

Our stay with the Lavorgnas confers a sweet, brief relief, the truth of Dad's death humming through me in intermittent twinges, like the feeling of grabbing an electric fence on a dare—first nothing, then a blunt pulse of pain, then your hand releases and it's nothing again. Occasionally I check the back window of Margie's block to see if the lights have come on in ours. Looking up at our dark windows, it's true. Going back into Margie's room, it isn't. Dad died, no he didn't, Dad died, no he didn't.

When we tire of "Orange-Colored Sky" we come out to the kitchen, where Mrs. Lavorgna feeds us a steamy helping of Mr. Lavorgna's famous spaghetti. Their table shrinks with the three of us there.

"How do you like working?" Cathy asks Margie's mother. This is the kind of thing Cathy asks adults all the time, as if she herself were fifty.

Mrs. Lavorgna smiles. "I like it." She works at Larry's Variety, one of a dozen thriving stores on Congress Street, in Rumford's business district.

"What do you do for your job?"

"I sell things," Mrs. Lavorgna says. "Then I take people's money and make change."

Nana sits in her usual spot, inscrutable. Now and again she murmurs something in Lithuanian. *Ash-ash, ticka-ticka.* . . . Maybe about us.

"What do you sell?" Cathy again.

"Oh . . . cigarettes and cigars."

"WHAT ELSE?" Betty now. She loves lists.

"Oh . . . candy."

"WHAT KIND?"

"Betty," I warn. But I want to know, too. Mrs. Lavorgna is the only working mother we know, and maybe we're all thinking the same thing: Will Mum have to work at Larry's now?

Mrs. Lavorgna names almost everything in the store, from Tootsie Rolls to toilet paper. Mr. Lavorgna names things Mrs. Lavorgna forgot. Nana listens to all this, in her chair, in her foreign-tongued silence, observing us the way she observes everything, as an alien entity on an unruly planet where she cannot quite believe she has landed.

"Where do you put your car?" Cathy asks, reading my mind. Dad's car is right next door to this block where we've been dropped for the evening; Dad's wonderful car just a few yards away, entombed in one of the Venskus garages. Nobody left to drive it. Nobody left to work. Will Anne have to give us all her money? We don't want Anne to have to give us all her money.

"I usually park on Congress Street," Mrs. Lavorgna says. Nana's giving us the eye — too many questions! But Cathy's question isn't about Mrs. Lavorgna's car. It's about Dad's car. Where will Mum park Dad's car? That is, if she gets a job at Larry's. And learns how to drive.

We're being rude—you're not supposed to interrogate adults—but no adult is going to call us on it. Certainly not these kindly people. Certainly not tonight. Mr. Lavorgna gives us two cookies each; we eat them in front of the TV, where Superman will perform a just-in-time feat of life-saving strength. We're in reruns, and I hope for the episode where Superman, after a rare failure to avert disaster, grabs the earth's surface, pulls hard, and turns back time. But it's not that one; it's the one where he stands there smiling at the bad guys while bullets bounce off him like gumdrops.

Will Mum sell gumdrops? When we come home from school, will Mum be at Larry's selling gumdrops? How lonely the kitchen will seem, the bird gibbering idly to no one, the chairs unoccupied, Mum not there until when—supper-time? bedtime? And then comes a larger, more terrifying thought—Mum not there at all. As Superman flies off, tri-umphant as usual, my welling eyes fix on the screen.

"What's the matter?" asks Margie. "Is it your father?"

I nod, but it's not Dad. Not exactly. I don't know what it is, exactly. I don't know that life hereafter will be filled with the threat of loss. All I know is that the impossible has hap-pened—my father is gone—which means that God could take my mother too.

After the lights in our house come on, we could easily walk home ourselves—kids walk all over the place in Mexico, unaccompanied, even after dark. But today is different, and here's Anne, arriving shortly after Superman flies off into the sunset, just as she said she would. She says something to Margie's parents, then thanks Margie—she always acknowl-edges children—and probably speaks to Nana, who prob-ably answers in a nod.

We turn left out the Lavorgnas' driveway, walk silent past

the Venskus block where yesterday Dad fell down dead. As we turn the corner at Miss Caliendo's, Cathy asks, "Who was there?"

"Lots of people. They came to pay their respects to Dad."

This turn of phrase is new to me. "Respects to Dad" sounds exactly right.

"LIKE WHO?" Betty always wants to know about the people.

"Well, like the Norkuses."

What? Our landlords—who shout *Make stop you jump!* when we kids run up the stairs too fast; our landlords to whom Dad paid rent once a week—they paid something to Dad? We walk in silence for a few more ticks.

"LIKE WHO ELSE?" Betty again.

Anne is holding Betty's hand, Betty's holding Cathy's hand, Cathy's holding my hand.

"Norma. And Mr. and Mrs. Hickey."

"WHO ELSE?"

"The Gallants." They live next door, old Mrs. Gallant and her grown daughters and grandkids, whom we play with. A household of women, which is what we are now.

"WHO ELSE?"

"Betty! Quit it!" Cathy. Me.

"It's all right. Let's see. The Gagnons, and the Dohertys, and the Fleurys, and the Witases and the Dons and the Fourniers."

Our neighbors. Who paid respects. To Dad. As we pass the Gagnons', pretty Mrs. Gagnon comes bounding out to murmur her *quel dommage;* we play with her girls and sometimes help her sew shoes in her parlor—piecework she brings home from the area shoe factories. Then it's turn left at the Dohertys', and here is Worthley Avenue and our driveway and there are the Norkuses in their lit-up kitchen window, he in an overshined suit jacket, she in her dress coat, a thick dark cloth thing, too heavy for the season, that hangs below her knees. Up we go, up we go, up we go, Anne in her church dress and us in our pedal pushers, and when we get to our door it opens into an altered place.

Mum is at the table, sitting again, still in her good dress and pearls. We're wild to see her, but she stares at us for a split second as if she's forgotten who we are. Then she wakes up, puts out her arms, kisses us one-two-three.

"Time for bed," she says, still sitting. After the heartwreck of the first day, the sustained shock of the news, the ordeal of the wake, she's composed herself for good and at great cost, and her body when I press myself against it feels like a gently closed door. It's been thirty-eight and a half hours. Any further tears—thousands, millions, in the years she has remaining of her own brief life—she will shed out of our sight.

Father Bob is still here, sitting next to the birdcage, breathing like a gut-shot deer. Mum looks up. "Father," she murmurs to her baby brother, "you're going to have to pull yourself together."

Another turn of phrase new to me, and it too sounds just right, for we have burst, haven't we? We lie in pieces that must be pulled together, and Father Bob has to help whether or not he believes he can. He will pull himself together because his big sister reminds him that he must. Tomorrow he must act as chief celebrant at the funeral Mass, his snow-white vestments signifying birth, not death. He must lead the Requiem prayer and sprinkle holy water on Dad's draped casket, and he will have to do this without breaking down.

Mum takes his coffee cup to the sink and he gets up. He puts one hand lightly on Mum's head; the other, fingers spread, hovers over the rest of us. *In nomine Patris . . .* he begins, blessing us all. I shut my eyes to receive God's grace. I pray for my uncle, who is still crying. We hug him good-bye—he'll stay the night in his room at Cumpy and Aunt Rose's house on Mexico Avenue—and then he, too, is gone.

So here we are, same as always, getting ready for bed as Anne lays out the new dresses we've worn only twice: last Sunday, and on Easter, the Sunday before that. We'll wear them again tomorrow to Dad's funeral. Anne helps us find our Easter hats. We're a working machine with a part missing. No Dad, just us, and the cats and the bird, and the Hickeys below, and the Norkuses below that, and the car with no driver, and the mill huffing and puffing on the bank, oblivious and aloof, the mill that gave Dad work and purpose and, quite possibly, the instruments of his death.

We wash our faces as we're told, brush our teeth, and recite our nightly prayers: the Our Father, the Hail Mary, the Angel of God, the Apostles' Creed, and the Act of Contrition.

"AHH FATHA," Betty begins. "WHO AHHT IN HEAVEN. HELLO BE THY NAME."

"That's wrong. She's saying it wrong."

"It's all right," Anne says. "Keep going, Bet."

"THY KINGDOM . . . COME . . . THY . . . THY . . . AHH FATHA . . ."

"Betty!"

"Be nice, you two. We can start with a Hail Mary."

Mum is in her bedroom, undressing in the dark—or maybe just sitting there in her good dress—wondering how to finish the awesome task of raising three more children, one of whom, at age eleven, can't advance past second grade or get her prayers straight.

"AHH FATHA . . ."

"That's not Hail Mary."

"She always says it wrong."

"God doesn't mind, Monnie."

We're draped over Anne the way we used to drape over Dad. Cathy on one side, I on the other, Betty in Anne's narrow lap. She smells like flowers, after an evening spent near the flower-choked coffin of a big-laughing, chain-smoking man who once taught her how to hem a skirt.

"Why don't we start all over, with the Our Father?" she asks us. "Everybody, now. 'Our Father, who art in heaven . . .'"

Our father—our actual father—art in heaven. Down here on earth, Anne is our calm. Our medicine. Our mirrour of grace and majestie divine.

Later that night, Cathy and I lie on our stomachs, ears pressed to the crack under our bedroom door, listening to Anne and Mum confer at the kitchen table a few feet from our pitcher-size ears. Betty stays in bed, good girl as always.

"I tried to see around to the back of his head." That's Mum, talking about Dad in his casket.

I can't make the leap, not even in my febrile imagination, to picture Dad lying there, eyes closed, voice gone, hands devoutly folded, a rosary twined through his work-chapped fingers. Even harder to imagine Mum squinting at his dead freckled head, craning to look for bruises suffered as he hit the Venskuses' blacktop.

"I couldn't see anything." That's Anne, confirming Mum's hope that it didn't hurt when he fell.

"Well," Mum sighs. "He was dead before he hit the ground." This is her comfort, repeated to all the visitors, repeated so often that I'll retain a permanent vision of Dad in slow motion, sliding open the garage door, pausing as if to hear a whisper from God, then dying quick, falling slow, and landing soft.

"He didn't suffer," Mum says. I hear the metallic clink of a teaspoon. "At least we have that."

Cathy nudges me. "What are they saying? Move over. I can't hear."

"Shh. It's about Dad."

Another clink, a sigh, and then a rustling. Mum is fiddling with the curtains, sounds like, at the kitchen window. What is she looking at? There's nothing to see at night but our neighbors' rooftops, and the lights along the river, the lit-up smokestacks and dark sky filling with Oxford clouds.

I hear Anne murmur something, her voice too low to catch—is she crying?

"Is she crying?" Cathy whispers. My sleeve is wet where her cheek rests against it.

"I don't know. Shh."

"Maybe it was the work," Mum says.

The man practically lives there, she used to say of Dad, who spent so much time at the mill, double shifts and triples, a wife and two children to care for, then three more girls.

The man practically lives there.

And now he doesn't.

I hear the curtains slide closed, green gingham curtains Mum bought and Dad liked. She's closing us inside, away from the steamy sky, away from those other families with working husbands, living fathers.

"It might have been the work," she says again.

My eyes sting but I'm too young to fully know why. That hushed note in my mother's voice is shame—the shame of widowhood: her husband gone *like that*. Gone, too, is our appearance as a family whole, gone the illusion of bounty, the sustaining tableau of a man with a lunch pail leaving 16 Worthley Avenue every morning and returning to that same address every night. Gone *like that*.

I hear a chair slide back, Mum getting up from the table—to go where? To her empty bed?

"Quick," Cathy says.

We scuttle to bed, still listening. The bathroom faucet goes on, then off. A faint splashing of water. Then the faucet goes on again. Cathy burrows nearer and we put our arms around each other. Her hair feels damp; our pajamas need washing. Then another quiet, feminine exchange of words behind the wall. The floorboards creak beneath their negligible weight.

After a moment of nothing, I hear another long, shame-shaded sigh from our mother.

It has been forty-one hours. We are changed. We are less.

3

Hiding

Dad's solemn requiem high mass has vanished, utterly, from my memory. I don't know where it went. Did I banish it myself, my nine-year-old mind deciding on the instant to evict the sight of my father's casket being ferried down the aisle of St. Theresa's? Or did it vanish eleven years later, after Mum's cancer death—her Mass replacing Dad's for all time, his incense and psalms replaced by her incense and psalms, her bells, her readings, her celebrant—Father Bob, again, his tears dripping down on her draped casket.

What does remain of Dad's funeral, vivid and urgent, is the afterwards: our kitchen filling once again with people. Dad's people, that is, the ones from Prince Edward Island—PEI, that rolling, sea-bound homeland of red earth, a place thick with lilacs and lore and Irish roots so deep Dad still said *daycent* for "decent" and *byes* for "boys" and *a-tall* for "at all." He'd colored our bedtime stories with characters

35

from that place, Jack and Paddy and a cast of supporting players whose names over time had become, like characters out of Dickens, a family shorthand for warnings, exemplars, qualities of habit.

Mertie McCormick, arriving on the doorstep "with one arm as long as the other," nothing for the table. Moral: Earn your keep.

Mrs. McCarn, grabbing the cap right off Dad's head to act out a story in which he appeared. Moral: The story is all in the telling.

The Kneebones, siblings who lived together in existential misery. If Gallacius were on fire and Templeton had a glass of water, Templeton would drink the water. Moral: Be nice to your sister.

Tell that one, Dad, we'd beg. *Tell the one about the Kneebones. Tell the one about Aunt Myrtle. Tell the one about John Quinn and the baked beans.* We loved imagining Dad's blue-sky farm, the ubiquitous dogs and cats, the potato blossoms and the mulish tractor, the guitar and fiddle music, the half-cracked neighbors who came and went. This was heritage, a chain made of words that had always felt a little like make-believe.

And now, astonishingly, here they are, Dad's actual people, gusting into our kitchen after the funeral like specters from that storied land. The Mitton girls, Dad's married nieces, gabby and wavy-haired, with their hats and pocketbooks and Mass cards; Dad's brother Fred in a threadbare Sunday jacket; Dad's sisters in their perfumed dresses. A burr in their *r*'s and red dust on their heels, the uncle patting our heads with his big bumpy hands, the aunts weeping and cupping our chins and clutching their clacketing rosaries.

"Would you look at Barry! Is he not the fill of his father's shirt!"

"And *this* one! The map of Ireland all over her face!"

"Merciful *God*, Margaret! The world still here and Albert not in it!"

Now Dad's the one in the stories. "Albert." "Uncle Albert." "The red fulla." Instead of being snuffed out like a spent cigarette, Dad's expanding, like the trail of smoke steaming up from his ashtrays, and the smoke goes everywhere.

One of the Mitton girls—the one who'd chosen Dad to walk her down the aisle—puts her pocketbook on a chair and reaches for me. "Your *father*," she says. She is hugely pregnant but manages to press me to her heart. "Your *father*." Her eyelashes are long and damp. "We loved Uncle Albert. We *loved* him."

Cathy and Betty, too, are being wonderfully smothered by emotional women who loved Dad. One of the aunts—Aunt Mae, short and bosomy and shaped like a popover—tries to hug us all three at once. "You *girls*," she cries. Her patting hands land on my back. "Albert's little girls."

Dad's people help Anne put out the food, they sweep the spring coats into our bedroom, they hug my mother over and over. I cannot listen hard enough; it's all such a wonder, all of Dad's stories, the same colors and exaggerations living again. Above the jabber of voices I catch a word or phrase pronounced in Dad's way, Dad's stories being told again. Once, near the end of the afternoon, I hear a brief, bracing note of laughter from Mum, a little shock from our old life.

Bit by bit, word by word, over the length of this fragile, disarranging day, I take in the remarkable fact that Dad had lived a life before me.

Then, evening: so suddenly quiet, the storybook characters gone, Anne and Mum murmuring once again in the kitchen—I'm left with the thought that I can't quite shake.

Dad was fifty-seven years old. I am nine.

On a sheet of Oxford paper I write the numbers, one over

the other, the minus sign in its proper place as Sister Ernestine showed us, "sloppy work" being a horror to the suffering eyes of Jesus.

57
-9

The number that results—48 years left over—cannot be right. Somehow, Dad had lived forty-eight years without me.

Cathy and Betty have fallen asleep. I sit on the floor of our bedroom in a patch of moonlight, wedged between the toy piano and a pile of schoolbooks, staring at the page. Dad was an adored baby brother who had learned his figures in a country schoolhouse, step-danced at parties, attended weekly Mass, fixed broken axles and milked a touchy cow, harvested potatoes and buried his parents and left the farm to try his luck in the mills of Maine. He took the ferry to New Brunswick and the train to Rumford in the middle of a life story that even then would not include me for another twenty-eight years.

One hundred percent of my life, all nine years, filled to the brim with Dad. How could I have figured so glancingly in his?

Addition is easier than subtraction. So I write different numbers. It has been sixty-one hours. After that, I count by days.

Come Monday, April 29, the start of our fifth day without Dad, we have to go back to school. Anne's bunk is neatly made up; her papers and grade books are gone. I smell oatmeal.

"We have to get up," Cathy whispers.

"I know. Betty, you awake?"

"NO."

"We have to," Cathy says.

"You first."

"No, you."

In the stillness we put on our uniforms. Cathy runs a comb through Betty's hair. We creep into the kitchen, use the bathroom in turn, come to the table without being told.

"I'm not hungry," I tell Mum when she puts my bowl in front of me.

Cathy: "Me neither."

The parakeet flutters down to eat with us. I run my finger over his smooth, feathered back. He's so tiny and warm; it's a miracle that a creature this small can look me in the eye.

"DO WE HAVE TO EAT?" Betty wants to know.

"Eat what you can," Mum says. "Try one bite."

She is fully dressed: plaid housedress with a snappy belt, skirt cut on the bias. How is she doing this? She moves slowly, as if under water, her eyes so swollen her eyelashes have nearly disappeared.

We take one bite each. One more. Then Mum takes our bowls, puts them in the sink. She urges the bird back into his cage. She finds our sweaters, one-two-three, and gentles us out the door.

"CAN'T WE STAY HOME?" Betty asks.

"No," Mum says tenderly. "You have to go."

"WHY?"

"I don't know," she tells us. "Because." Her voice is wavy and hoarse, a pitch lower than normal. Has she slept at all since it happened?

We descend the stairs mousily (no *Make stop you jump!* from the Norkuses), bend to pat Tootsie as Dad surely had, and head to school together, doing our good-girl duty, shoulders bumping, avoiding the silence of our friends.

In my fourth-grade classroom, I file through the door

with my classmates and slide into my seat. Is Sister Ernestine looking at me? I hope not. Instead, to my great relief, she asks us all to stand, as usual.

"*Bonjour, mes enfants,*" she says, as usual.

"*Bonjooour, ma Soeur,*" we say, as usual.

She asks us to recite the Lord's Prayer, as usual, and then to sit down, as usual. She begins with Religion, as usual. She says nothing about Dad.

Sister Ernestine, memorable and kind, divides our days into discrete units designed to deliver relief to children who are good at some things and bad at others. After Religion comes Geography; Sister moves straight to Ferdinand Magellan, the explorer whom we read about last week.

"Mr. Magellan, you will recall, lost his parents at the age of ten—" A silence. Sister stops, clears her throat. I drop my gaze to my desk and leave it there. "But because he had an illustrious family," she says, moving quickly now, "he was sent to the royal court to serve as a page to the queen." I fixate on the surface of my desk, a hundred initials and ink marks scrubbed over and sanded out and defaced anew, generations of fiddlers and doodlers before me. The room falls quiet again. I hear the snap of the pull-down map, the tap of Sister's pointer.

"Where was Magellan born?"

Sabrosa, Portugal, I say to myself.

"Portugal," somebody says.

"To what kind of family?"

Illustrious, I say to myself.

"Industrious," somebody says.

"And Mr. Magellan was the first explorer to do what?"

Cross all the meridians of the globe, I say to myself.

Sister waits.

Cross all the meridians of the globe, I silently urge somebody to call out. But nobody knows. My face burns from the inside out, for I can feel the prickle of my classmates' gaze as they look to me. This is my kind of answer: an exact copy of the homework reading.

"To cross . . ." Sister says. "Anybody? To cross all the . . . ?"

"Countries?"

"No."

"Bridges?"

"No."

"Crosses?"

"For heaven's sake, no. Monica?"

"Meridians of the globe," I murmur, tender explosions of shame erupting everywhere. Face, toes, everywhere. *Run,* I think. *Hide!* But where?

"Thank you, Monica."

Sister Ernestine moves on, recapping Mr. Magellan's fearless voyage and pointing out the strait that bears his name. I imagine the man at the prow of his ship, heart-shook but determined, chin lifted against the usual dreads: death by mutiny, death by scurvy, death by storm or shark or rogue wave, death by unreceptive natives. Sister normally skips these inconveniences, ending all explorers' tales the same way: discoveries galore, everybody safe. But I read the whole chapter last week, not just the half-page assignment, so I know what nobody else knows: Magellan died on the island of Mactan, his body savagely pierced by iron spears.

He would have died anyway. Eventually. Of something. Even if he'd made it to the unheard-of age of one hundred, he'd be dead now; many hundreds more years had passed since then. These men who made memorable journeys, discovered fountains of youth and stores of gold and America itself—they all died in the end. In my newfound terror of the mystery of mortality, it is Magellan, the explorer with the gemlike name, who will keep me awake nights imagining death—my own, everyone's. Forever after I'll conflate the image of Magellan gliding over the straits in his ship with Dad moving down Mexico Avenue on his own last voyage.

Everybody dies. And despite our daily preparations to meet God in eternity, I seem to be the only one in my class who knows this.

I have to get up for lunch, join a line, walk to the cafeteria. I follow my feet, still looking down, over the scarred floors and stray crumbs; I drop into my seat and stare at the bag; and open the bag; and eat what's there. All around me the din of children with fathers. All around me, regular life, which is loud, which smells. Egg smell from the bag lunches, swampy smell from the hot lunches, a whiff of kid-sweat. Cathy and Betty eat at the second-grade table, way over; I can't look. My vision shrinks to a small, private circle—the table, the bag, my egg sandwich—and then a hand slides into that circle, the hand of my friend Denise, who passes a cookie to me, a Toll House her mother made special. I grab it, I eat it, I don't look up.

In Arithmetic, my classmates have moved a step beyond the long division Dad helped me with on the night before he died; now we're working multidigit problems that render me mute with shock. Five days ago I understood it all, Dad scratching his pencil over my paper back when the world, like arithmetic, obeyed the rules. Now, I sit at my desk squinting down at too many numbers, wishing people really could vanish into thin air, as Cathy had so briefly done.

My hair is red and my cheeks freckled like Dad's—"the map of Ireland all over her face." But in the classroom I'm not only the sole redhead but the sole Monica in an era of Debbies and Lindas and Karens and Pams, and my very name feels like a neon hat. I'm the girl whose father died—*dropped*, people said, as if describing an apple falling from a tree; Dad, our shiny apple, *dropped*, and now I'm one of three fatherless children in the entire school. The other two are back in Sister Edgar's second-grade classroom, one of them struggling with a pair of knitting needles, the other writing a letter to Mum, trying to close the distance between now and last bell, when we will all three run headlong home to find her still living.

For three weeks, day by inching day, we leave Mum in the morning, our oatmeal half eaten. Seven hours later we return to her at a gallop, finding her resting on one of our beds. We sit on the covers and tell her we're home. She looks at us, she listens. Cathy learned her times-fours; I liked my sandwich; Betty saw a bird. We bring her these things as if they were frankincense and myrrh. Then she gets up, busy at the stove by the time Anne gets home from the high school.

Every few days another neighbor drops off a casserole. Mrs. Hickey from downstairs, the Gallant ladies next door. Mum's friendly with the other mothers, but she doesn't have a circle of close lady friends, not even within her family; her father and sister live a block away but her job is not to be their pal but their pillar. When Dad was living she'd gone to Mass and Benediction, parents' night, the church fair, meetings of the Sodality of the Immaculate Conception. But mostly, like us, she waited every day—in the busy, chore-filled, aromatic shelter of our bright, packed rooms—for Dad to come home for supper. The Gallant ladies linger a bit, they speak kindly, they squeeze her hands, but this is the era before "closure," before "letting it out," an era of private mourning. You don't say things out loud. Mum, a shell-shocked widow trying to find her footing, intends to keep her misery to herself.

She isn't sleeping. One night I wake with a start—everything eerily calm, Cathy asleep next to me, Betty asleep in her bunk, Anne, softly breathing, asleep in hers. I slip out of bed and listen: nothing. I crack open our bedroom door and find the kitchen empty, everything in silhouette: the table and chairs, the sewing machine, the birdcage. Nothing breathes; even the cats have vanished. Then I hear something—at least I think I do, a sound nearly eroded from memory, something that might be a voice, or a motion, or a thought.

Is it Dad? In there, in the parlor? One step, then another, and I'm at the parlor doorway, peering in. I see a human shadow in the darkness. Blood rushes through my ears, I can no longer place the sound I either did or did not hear, and then the figure resolves into the motionless shape of my mother.

Standing in the center of the room, she fumbles with her nightgown as if she's just put it on. What is she doing? What time is it? I do not understand the thing to which I'm bearing witness: a widow awake in her too-small house, unwilling to return to her marriage bed. Like a spirit from the ghost stories she and Dad loved to tell, she haunts her own house at night, and as soon as it empties out in the morning she sleeps at last, borrowing beds that smell of her children.

She hears me. Turns. Her beautiful brown eyes meet me in the dark.

"Mumma?" I whisper.

She doesn't answer. I'm not positive she can see me. I've intruded on something adult and private, and so, not knowing what else to do, I retreat gently, as if backing away from

44

a strange but benign-looking animal, my eyes still fixed on hers. By morning it feels like a dream.

Twenty-nine days now without Dad. We come home from school, a bright, late-May day, to find Mum already up. "Where's Betty's paper?" she asks.

"What paper?"

She'd been watching us from the window, her girls coming home from school, Cathy and I toting book bags and pencils and papers marked *A*.

"Didn't I see a paper in her hand? Just now?"

This isn't the first time Mum has seen a paper where none exists. Betty never has a paper. Not an arithmetic paper not a name-the-explorers paper not a religion paper not a spelling paper not a vocabulary paper. In the six school years that have taken her only to second grade, not once has Betty come home with a paper. But sometimes Mum sees a paper anyway, wishful thinking she'd surely discussed with Dad, who shared Mum's worry for their eternal second-grader who could knit but not purl, who could not add two and two or reliably spell *cat*. More than one well-meaning meddler had suggested a home for the "feeble-minded," a place to unburden us all of the bruised fruit of Mum's womb. Mum and Dad had met these well-wishers with equal parts fire and ice: Betty would grow up with us, go to school with us, make her First Communion and Confirmation like any other Catholic child, be our big sister as long as she could, and our forever little sister after that. Mum and Dad had decided that, together.

"I thought she had a paper," Mum says.

I would give anything—all the cats, all my *A*'s, my immortal soul—to will a paper into Betty's hand. A paper with a big fat *A-plus*. A big fat *Excellent work, Elizabeth!* Mum's eyes look wounded and wet. *Don't go back to bed, Mum*, I think. *Stay up, with us.*

Somehow, she opens a drawer. Somehow, she pulls out a baking pan. Somehow, she asks us, "How does banana bread sound?"

A few days after that—the brilliant weather still holding—we come home to find her not only up, but in the bathroom unraveling her pin curls. She hasn't been out of the house once since Dad died except for Sunday Mass and once, yesterday, to have her hair freshly blued. Because today she has to go to the bank.

The three of us crowd her at the sink to watch this palliative scene, Mum making herself pretty again. Putting on her lipstick, she begins to look more like our real mother—a petite, cushiony, dimpled, doe-eyed woman with milky skin and prematurely gray hair.

Cathy pats her hair. "Mumma, you look beautiful."

Mum blots her lips on a Kleenex. "I'm going out to meet my public," she says. This is her best joke, a leftover from her old vibrant self.

Only it's not a joke anymore. The "public" is watching. We follow her into the kitchen, where she opens the cupboard and takes an envelope from the gravy boat—her first check from the United States government.

"If it wasn't for FDR," she tells us, "I'd be out scrubbing floors."

She has said this a dozen times since Dad died. *If it wasn't for FDR, I'd be out scrubbing floors.* She means the New Deal, of course, enacted to protect families just like ours. But she doesn't explain; perhaps she finds it embarrassing. All

I know in this hastening moment, my mother hiding the check in her big white purse, is this: FDR is a dead president to whom we are meant to be grateful. I'm used to loving the president we have now—the Irish Catholic President Kennedy—because Mum has taught us to love him. His wind-blown hair, his Hyannis tan, his pity for the poor. She refers to him as "Jack" and loves that he won't wear a hat in the cold. She can quote from his inauguration speech. And she looks for news of him: his weekly trips to Mass with Jackie and the children; his dealings with the old, ugly, hatchet-faced Khrushchev (those poor Russians, with a president who looks like that!); his cultured Boston accent, whose wide *a*'s sometimes creep into her own speech. She loves the backlighted shots of him cavorting with the kids despite his bad back; the shots of all those birthdays and Catholic holidays, a whole packload of Kennedys laughing around a table, their houses adorned, like ours, with a crucifix or a picture of the Sacred Heart. "Jack's one of a kind," Mum likes to say, but now there is this other president, this long-gone FDR, to whom we are indebted, so I try to love that president, too, and thank him in my prayers.

"You girls stay put," Mum says. "Anne will be home before long." Anne with her papers and grade books, her dear, rich, healing presence. Mum's best friend now. Whatever time she gets back from school won't be soon enough.

Mum gives us a look. "No bickering."

She means Cathy and me: *that's mine no it isn't yes it is,* our predictable loop of complaint born of being so closely quartered. *You're copying me no I'm not yes you are.* It seems wrong to act like this with Dad gone, but we do it anyway, ashamed that we've managed to wait mere days before reprising our trivial wrangles.

47

"CAN I GO?" Betty always wants to go with Mum, and Mum cannot refuse her.

She hesitates. "All right. Put on a sweater." Betty is too skinny and always cold.

So they start out, the two of them, down the stairs, Mum with her lipstick and Betty in her school uniform, out into the brightness. Once on the street, Mum puts her hand to her hair and plumps it up. She has polished her shoes and cleaned her eyeglasses with vinegar and soaked her rings in ammonia. This vanity is not silly or merry or self-indulgent; rather, it is necessary. My mother is trying, as far as it is still possible, to resemble a married woman who packs her husband's lunch every morning and puts half his weekly paycheck into a savings account. She dreads appearing otherwise, and if this means paying to have her hair blued once a week from here to eternity, then so be it.

She moves down Gleason Street in her pretty shoes, a white cardigan, a pink dress I like. She holds Betty's hand. She walks the two blocks to the bank, where the tellers know all our names. There, my mother removes her first Social Security check from her white pocketbook. The teller, the daughter of one of our neighbors, says, "I'm sorry for your loss." She instructs Mum to flip the check over; she has to sign. Mum flips the check over, finds the line that says sign. Now, in her careful, fine, Palmer-method handwriting, my mother writes *Margaret Mary Wood*. Right in front of everybody.

FDR's check comes as a palpable relief to my mother, but relief, like life now, is a paradox. On one hand, Mum takes great pains to prove she has not been left destitute—as indeed she has not; she saved Dad's money, and they might have kept a small life-insurance policy. Nothing obvious changes. She rises from her afternoon sleep to bake something rich every day; she bleaches our blouses to make them look new; she gives us money for weekly "hot lunch," money for sno-cones, money to save the pagan babies. On the other hand, if we look too cared for, or she shows herself with a fresh perm or new shoes, then it stands to reason that we've got money to burn, and then, of course, the Norkuses could raise the rent beyond our ability to pay, and bang we're out on the street, atoning for Mum's grand deception, shoeless waifs selling used pencils while our dead-eyed mother toils in somebody else's house buffing the baseboards. (Whose house would that be? What family of our acquaintance has a hired floor scrubber?)

Nobody—not one person—in our town lives on the street. But Mum isn't kidding. Reasonable or not, "scrubbing floors" is her fear.

I absorb these fears during our first fragile weeks without Dad, keeping up my own appearances by brushing my teeth in a military right-left precision, parting my hair with a wetted comb. I'm timid in any case—"desperate odd," Dad always said, which meant shy—but now I have something big and bright and lumbering: a deceased father. The only solution: Lie low. Lower. Be a good girl. Do everything the nuns say. Get your homework in not early, not late, but exactly on time. Uniform skirt smoothed before sitting down, smoothed again before standing up. Look normal. Look normal. Look normal.

Just as May turns to June, the weather prematurely hot, Sister Ernestine surprises our class by taking us outside for lunch and sitting splat on the ground, flipping back her veil like a ponytailed teenager. We sing something religious as grace, then eat our lunches on our laps, picnic-style. I pick at my bologna sandwich, watch a game of jump rope that

I decline to join, sit on the grass with my feet straight out, ankles politely crossed.

At day's end, Sister keeps me after school. It's not, as far as I know, my turn to do *le ménage*—clapping the erasers outside, washing the blackboard, lining up used chalk by size. I come to the front of the room and wait, uneasy. Sister Ernestine is plump and short-limbed, not much taller than I, in fact is a good bit shorter than the tallest nine-year-old in the class. What can she possibly want? Zero chance that I neglected my homework, or talked out of turn, or allowed my eyes to stray briefly to the paper of my neighbor. Has she guessed that Cathy and I sneaked up the embankment behind the convent last fall to snicker at the dowdy white undies flapping on a clothesline? Does she know we peeked into the cellar windows and saw her roller-skating in the basement?

"Your daddy . . ." she begins, and my stomach drops, and her eyes well, and I stand in an icy terror. She's going to *talk about it.* But I hold her gaze anyway, because I love her. She's old, I believe, though it's hard to tell—in those ponderous garments the nuns look no age at all. Her hairline, what I can see of it beneath her starched headgear, shows as a glint of silver, and she wears rimless glasses that sit atop her apple cheeks and jounce a bit when she talks.

"Your daddy," she stammers again, the tears now coursing freely down her cheeks, "was called home to God."

"Yes, Sister."

Her hands are hidden inside her blousy black sleeves; her forehead pearls with sweat. Her chestnut-size rosary beads belt her at the waist, a silver cross dangling like Marley's clankety chains, all the accouterments of her faith unshakably displayed as she faces me with reddening eyes in front of the map of the world. Back in September she'd pointed out the big bright country of Mexico, then traced her finger across a whole continent to find the piddling speck that was us.

"God wanted your daddy . . ."

"Yes, Sister." Look normal. Look normal. Look normal.

" . . . to come home to Him . . ."

"Yes, Sister," I whisper, gulping now, lost to her sympathy.

"God called him home . . ." She pauses, shaking her head; has she misplaced her point?

I gaze at her, then at my shoes. I ask the only question I have, the only question anyone has. It takes all my breath: "Why?"

She lays a hand on my shoulder. "For no reason I can fathom," she tells me. "No reason at all, Monica."

I pause, taking in my own name. "Yes, Sister."

She closes her eyes. "Your poor mother. Your poor, poor mother."

My poor mother. Despite her blued hair and pretty shoes and secret sleeping hours, her fear has come true: pity even from the nuns, who consider personal suffering a grace from God.

We used to rush him at the door, elbowing each other to get there first, cleaving to his scent, to the solid living fact of him, to his haw-haw-haw laughter.

"YOU'RE A BIG FAT EGG!" This was Betty's only joke and she milked it for years.

Dad put on his fake frowny face and flapped his jowls. "*What* did you call me?"

"A BIG FAT EGG!"

Frownier, jowlier: "*What* did you call me?"

The three of us: "HAHAHAHAHAHAHA!"

He sat on our bed at night, Cathy and Betty and I nestling

against the time-softened flannel of his shirt, his presence a smoky, masculine mystery amid our dolls and hair bands and pink pajamas. One of the Oxford's specialties was "fine book paper," yet we didn't own many books; instead, Dad told stories, his voice deep and smoke-scratched and lilted with an Island brogue. *Once upon a time there was a fulla*, a Dad story might begin. *A desperate-handsome young fulla, all huthery and poverized, no money a-tall, foostering through the neighbor's garbage can....* This "fulla" would turn out to be one of his boyhood neighbors, or else a prince in disguise—Dad always left the outcome in doubt. But if a princess showed up, we knew her "fearful-grand" beauty by the vividness of Dad's words, words I adored because they belonged to our family.

"How old was your father?" people asked. Sister Ernestine. The clerk at Nery's. Our pastor, Father Cyr.

"Fifty-seven."

"Oh, so young," they said, shaking their heads. "So young."

But Dad wasn't young; strangers mistook him for our grandfather. Besides, I'd done the math: forty-eight years he'd lived before me. Maybe he, like Mum, believed God had delivered three extra children, one-two-three, as a sign of His plan for this couple's long, long friendship. But God had also delivered to him the Oxford Paper Company, and the foamy river it sat upon. And the long working hours it required. And the poison it put in the air. Three more girls from God might portend a long married life, but a multi-acre paper mill, with much heat but no heart, could make for stiff competition if it decided to bestow the opposite.

Maybe it was the work.

Dad at the wheel. Dad in his chair. Dad on the steps with his lunch pail. Dad walking Mum to church. Look at the husband and wife. Look at the parents and children. Our life had been so mercifully predictable. So open to the light.

Now every day we come home to our mother waking. "Mum? I saw a bird." Every day she rises, puts on her glasses, tries to look like everybody else. Our third floor feels like the teetering top of a tower, the five of us hiding with our brushed teeth and clean clothes and washed faces, at the mercy of whoever, or whatever, might decide to give us one more good hard shake.

4

Explorers

I N EARLY JUNE, thirty-six days after Mum tells Father Bob he'll have to "pull himself together" for the funeral, my uncle makes a surprise visit to my classroom at St. Theresa's.

"Why, look, children!" gasps Sister Ernestine. "Look who's here!"

Father Bob's appearance makes me feel like St. Juan Diego finding roses blooming in winter. For the first time since Dad died I look up from my desk, feverish with relief, leaping to my feet along with my classmates.

"Bonjooour, mon Père!"

"Bonjour, mes enfants." He strolls to the front of the room, the hem of his swishing cassock lightly webbed with cat hair, his own hair pomaded into a shiny widow's peak, his fresh-shaven cheeks scented with Aqua Velva. Though I don't understand what an effort this is, I do see that his face isn't

exactly his face, that his grin is something he's hauled up from somewhere deep for this occasion.

Sister Ernestine takes his hat and then sits down to hide her swooning. Father Bob observes the class for a loaded moment, arms akimbo, his shiny shoes tapping as if in impatience. What will he say? The suspense is exquisite. Will he advise us, as Father Cyr does, to live a life of loving kindness? Will he bring announcements, as Father LaPlante often does, about the church fair or First Friday Mass or the schedule for Confirmation?

"Boys and girls," he says. "What's new?"

Everybody laughs. This is so, so funny! Father wants to know what's new!

Nyew is how he says it, because he is splendidly educated and *nyew* is how they pronounce this word in England. He also says *pro*-gress, with a long *o*. Possibly he does this more with Dad gone. It drives Mum crazy. *Quit putting on airs*, she used to chide him, but as a priest he's allowed to put on all the airs he cares to. He was born loving words and works them like a paint kit.

Father Bob makes no special note of me except for a quick, sidelong glance that says: *I know you're here*. This makes me a hundred times more exceptional than if he'd announced to the class, *There's my niece*. He does this when visiting Cathy and Betty's classroom, too, roving the room, singling out our friends instead of us, which is far more delicious, our glory deflecting to other kids who become celebrities once removed. The ones who didn't have the smarts to want Betty's friendship will now pay.

"Denise Vaillancourt, how are you this morning?"

"Fine, Father. Thank you, Father."

"Margie Lavorgna, I saw your father when I stopped at Fisher's just now. He's looking well. Such an affable fellow."

56

"Thank you, Father."

I remind myself to look up *affable* and tell Margie what it means.

"You'll give your mother my very best regards?"

Very best regards! Nobody we know says "very best regards"!

"Yes, Father. Thank you, Father."

He has this way of sounding simultaneously chummy and formal, making a child the delectable center of something rare and memorable.

"Sister, what are the children studying today?"

"We're studying the explorers, Father." Sister Ernestine swans across the room, pulls down the map of the world, and asks Judy Pepin to point out Portugal, and Spain, and Italy. Then, in case Father prefers a more contemporary show-and-tell, she asks Penny Naples to point out the neighborly provinces of Canada and the godless expanse of the U.S.S.R. She does not consult the boys, who can't be trusted to come up with the right answers on cue.

"Well done. Very, very well done." Father beams at the child who has pointed correctly—but really he's beaming at me. "Excellent pro-gress."

I sit there, thinking: *Mine, mine, mine.*

"Very nice visiting with you, Sister. Thank you."

"Oh, thank *you,* Father!" She raises a single eyebrow at us, whereupon we leap once again to our feet.

"Au revoir et merci, mon Père!"

He shows his small, white hands and down go our heads, down, down, down, a domino-quick reflex.

"In nomine Patris," he intones, *"et Filii, et Spiritus Sancti."*

We cross ourselves. "Amen."

His custom is to visit all the grades, not just ours, and then drive home to Mum and wait for us. As we file to the cafeteria for lunch, I spot him through the great doors. He's sitting in his parked car, his hands on the wheel, his forehead gently resting on his hands. After lunch, filing past the door again, I look for his car and it's gone.

So he's with Mum now, and here's what I want to imagine as I finish my first good-tasting lunch in weeks: the brother and sister as their old selves, playing a ferocious round of Scrabble in the kitchen, Mum registering challenges until she can't take one more ridiculous, unheard-of, perfectly legal English word pointed out in Father's Bob's take-along dictionary. She dawdles so long over sorting her letters that her baby brother groans in fake, theatrical anguish. *Maaargaret!*

Keep your shirt on. I've got something. She's angling for a seven-letter word but so far that's happened only once.

If you had something, you'd have played it—he checks his handsome watch—*twenty minutes ago.*

Her cheeks pinken, she gives him a catlike leer, then lays down tile after tile. I imagine that S-I-N-G-I-N-G is the magic word, the *g* shared with Father Bob's triple-word-scored *ghost.*

La la la, Mum says. *Don't get too big for your britches, buster.*

But that's not what will happen today when he goes to her. The Scrabble game will sit on the table, unopened. She'll pour him some coffee. He'll cry and cry. Mum will watch for us out the window, coming down the street in our green uniforms. "The girls are here, Father," she'll say when she spots us. And he'll pull himself together.

As soon as Father Bob leaves our classroom in a gust of glory, Sister Ernestine says, "Let's stick with Geography." She's feeling good, flushed with secondhand celebrity, so instead of moving on to French, Geography it is. Her favorite.

She's mad about explorer stories, all those brazen men from Spain and Portugal in storm-shocked fleets they named for saints, their intrepid forays to convert the heathen masses while dumping their ballast of rocks and replacing it with gold, tea, saffron, curry. But the Europeans aren't the only characters in her collection; still agog from Father's visit, she unveils one of her favorites, a real corker about the Oxford's founder, a story that unfolded "right here in our own backyard" about eighty years before she assigned us our permanent, scarified desks in her fourth-grade classroom. Every schoolchild in Mexico learns this story, which goes like this:

On a snow-blown December day in 1882, a young, well-fed Portland businessman—Mr. Chisholm was his name—arrived by train at the Rumford Point Hotel, borrowed a sleigh from the proprietor, and started down the road along the river. What could he be up to? As he made his purposeful way, the snow magically lifted and the day turned clear and crisp and still. The man enjoyed this quality of quiet, for he was an industrialist whose daily life teemed with enterprise. The cold sun poured over this blessed quiet, until a remarkable thundering left the man no doubt of his location. Out of the sleigh he climbed, his eyebrows grizzled with hoarfrost. He shivered inside his heavy coat, ran a glove along the country-bred nose of his borrowed horse, slipped the beast a sugar cube for its trouble.

"What was the horse's name?"

A beat. "St. Jude."

"Really?"

"Well, the Chisholms were Catholic." (Like all of Sister's explorers, whether or not the evidence supported the claim.)

"But he borrowed the horse."

"Then I assume the hotel man was also Catholic."

In the bracing cold, the stranger's breath formed cloudlets of wonder as he took in the river's first plummet, a nearly perpendicular drop of seventy-five feet that split a wild expanse of land ringed by snow-muffled hills. His gaze traveled downriver, where the Androscoggin continued its plunge, one hundred eighty feet over a half-mile stretch, the rocks and boulders smoothed over time by the river's inestimable weight. Here was Hugh J. Chisholm, our town's industrial founder, standing on high like God at the beginning of the world, the sound of falling water and a new idea drumming in his head.

The horse rattled its furry ears. The winter light rinsed the scene with a nearly painful clarity. The wilderness rolled away, and away, until Hugh believed he could see all the way to Canada.

He'd grown up near Niagara and knew at once: The Rumford falls rivaled that legendary length.

"How did he measure it?"

"By eye."

"How can you—?"

"He was brilliant, children. *Brilliant.*"

A calculating man, Mr. Hugh J. Chisholm, Canadian-born son of a Scottish scholar. In a less capricious world, our Hugh might have become a scholar himself, but his father's untimely end—drowned after tumbling off a steamer from Toronto—sent the heart-rattled son into the working world at the age of thirteen.

Another fatherless explorer. But this time nobody looks at me. Father Bob's visit has shifted the burden of pity from me to young Hugh. I listen along with everyone else, my chin lifted toward the story of us.

"How do you fall off a steamer?" somebody asks.

"He was a scholar. I suppose he was reading a book."

After digging potatoes for two soul-numbing days, young

Hugh turned to selling newspapers on the Toronto-Detroit rail line with another boy, name of Thomas Edison, a kindred spirit, fellow genius, and lifelong friend.

"And Thomas Edison, you'll remember, was the inventor of . . . ?"

"The cotton gin!"

"No."

"The Stanley Steamer!"

"No."

"The telescope?"

"Children, this was your homework *two weeks* ago. Monica?"

"The electric light."

"Thank you."

Hugh saw something in paper that brainy Thomas missed. By the time he beheld the unharnessed power of the Rumford falls, Hugh was a seasoned capitalist used to the long view. Well supplied with cigars, he lingered at the summit. Standing a little, walking a little. His boots made pacing traces in the crystallizing snow. He did this for more than an hour. More than two.

"Where was he?"

"At the top of Falls Hill. Only it wasn't Falls Hill then. It was just a little path overlooking that raging waterfall."

Beyond the deafening miracle of the falls, there really wasn't much to see on that wintry day. No sign of human striving but a trifling wreck of a gristmill, a smaller sawmill weathered to the bone. The sun-spangled water ribboning between Rumford and Mexico existed mostly unseen and unknown, a geysering thunder already changing shape in Hugh's thrumming mind. He climbed back into the borrowed sleigh, afire with plans.

"And his plan was . . . what, children?"

Everybody knows this one: "The mill!"

Did he imagine the smokestacks, the woodyards, the whistle that would alert generations of children to the hour of nine in the morning? Did he envision the logjammed canal, the footbridges and savings banks, the sidewalks and church steeples, the dress shops and the bowling alley, schools brimming with smart, ambitious children? Did he foresee the great steam cloud pumping like a signal at the heart of the valley, pumping like a heart itself, a heart made of sulphur and smoke?

"Well?" Sister asks. "Did he?"

"Yes!"

"And why is that?"

"Because he was an explorer!"

"And explorers have what?"

"Courage!"

"And what else?"

"Goals!"

"And what else?"

"Imagination!"

On the return trip, about a quarter mile from the hotel, St. Jude—who cared nothing for industrial daydreams and much for dinner in a well-stocked livery—bolted up a half-frozen hill, upsetting the sleigh and all its contents, including our town's imagineer, now splatted on the ice with an additional shivery hour to ruminate on the glorious possibility of "building a city in the wilderness." As the hard ground slowly numbed his hind parts, he thought of his old friend Thomas down there in his bright, warm workshop in Menlo Park, New Jersey, angling a way to deliver light to the masses.

We laugh at the picture: our portly founder, flat on his backside.

"That's humility," Sister says. But she's laughing, too. "No success without failure, children. First you have to fall flat down."

Hugh got up from that frozen ground and spent the next decade secretly buying all the land along the river. And lo, it came to pass: A city in the wilderness did indeed rise up, year by year, dam by dam, canal by canal, turbine by turbine, mill by mill, block by block—blocks like ours, filling with workers now coming in by the trainload.

In they went, over the footbridges to mills flourishing on Chisholm land. "To the Rumford Falls Paper Company, which made—?"

"Newsprint!"

"And the Rumford Falls Sulphite Company?"

"Sulphite pulp!"

"And the International Paper Company?"

"Manila, envelope paper, newsprint, and writing paper!"

"And the Continental Paper and Bag Company?"

"Bags and envelopes!"

And finally, on the land where the river made its elbow bend into Mexico, the Oxford Paper Company, Hugh's ruby of modern papermaking, an innovation that eventually enfolded its sister mills and met what its founder rightly predicted as an exploding twentieth-century demand for books and magazines. With the modern century barely under way, our once drowsy, vacated valley had been fully remade as an industrial powerhouse of more than ten thousand lucky, multitongued, deeply grateful souls, their fortunes tied forever to a Canadian immigrant and his headlong dreams.

"And at some point along the way," Sister tells us, "your own fathers stepped onto a Rumford train platform and joined their number."

She waits for the ending to sink in, a little twist we haven't heard before. All year Sister has told this explorer story and others, their embedded lessons accumulating thusly: Be brave. Set goals. Use your imagination.

But today the lesson is this: We live in a town made remarkable by the work of our fathers. Today she tells this story just for me.

A few mornings later, Mum picks up the ringing phone as we get ready for school.

Only two days left of our nun-dictated routine; the looming of summer, that upcoming season of free time, feels for the first time ever like a saddling weight. Too many hours to fill, and the only foreseeable balm is our big sister hearing our prayers at day's end. How many days does summer hold? I've tried to count them out but they're too abundant to hold in my head, just as the count of Dadless days has at last gotten away from me. Fifty-four days, fifty-six days, the numbers piling up too fast now, relentless and unruly. I have to count by weeks instead—nearly eight of them so far, a smaller sum that makes Dad seem a little less far away.

"Is it just talk?" Mum says to someone on the line. She means the strike talk wildfiring around town: contract negotiations coming up, three unions suddenly battling for the right to rep the rank and file.

Cathy snatches up the parakeet and swings him around by the tail, which he never seems to mind, but her laughter, and Betty's, makes it hard to hear. "Shh," I tell her. "Put him back. Get your skirt on."

"It's probably just talk," I hear Mum say again. "A few flapjaws stirring up trouble." Who is she talking to? Our brother? Is he worried about a strike?

My family is collapsing like a pile of sticks because we can't believe Dad's gone; why wouldn't the mill, where Dad spent so much of his time, be doing the same? Because I am nine years old and willing to believe anything, I believe Dad's death has changed Hugh Chisholm's mill. Its constant sighing finds me in my bed at night; in the daytime I lift my chin, avert my gaze. I can't bear to look at it, to smell it, to hear its heavy breath. With Dad not in it, the Oxford suddenly looks like a factory.

Mum hangs up but doesn't look worried. She doesn't look anything. The world isn't getting through. "Who was that?" I ask her.

"Nobody."

"Was it Barry?"

"Put that poor creature down," Mum says to Cathy. "I mean it."

"Mum?" I persist. "Is there gonna be a strike?" Sister Ernestine has a thing for English words and the tricks they play. She loves homographs and synonyms and sometimes teases us to spell words backwards. As far as I can make out, the word *strike* is an *antagonym*, Sister Ernestine's word for a word that means both itself and its opposite. Like *buckle*, which means to fasten and secure, or to implode and collapse. Like *cleave*, which means to brutally split apart, or to cling together.

Strike means to hit something, but also to walk away from something—your job—so you don't get hit.

"Mum? Mumma? Is there going to be a strike?"

She shakes her head, rifling the hall coat rack for our sweaters. "The men in Manhattan can't afford one." Is this what Barry said on the phone? "Cathy, put him *down*. Where's your skirt?"

"Mum? What men in Manhattan?"

"The men who own the mill."

I don't know what to say. I'd thought *Dad* owned the mill.

65

Dad and all the fathers. The mill manager's visit had been my first clue; now this.

"Are you sure? About the strike?"

"Don't be a worrywart," Mum says. "Nobody's going on strike. Betty, here's your milk money. Right here in your pocket. Don't lose it."

"Mum? How do you know nobody's going on strike? Mumma? How do you know—?"

"Because Dad said so." She sighs. "Now get your shoes on."

What? Does she mean Dad said this when he was still living, or that he said so just now? On the phone? Is there some way to speak to him that is known to everyone but me?

"Mum—?"

"*Now*. Get your shoes on."

During Religion lesson, Sister Ernestine stuffs us with advice about how to retain our Catholic Conduct over the unfettered months of summer. I stare out the door-size windows of our classroom at the sky filled with real and man-made clouds. The Oxford's work is never done—that's what Dad always said. It runs on a three-shift schedule, around the clock, around the year, halting only for Christmas and the Fourth of July, and even then a skeleton crew goes in to keep the machines running. Otherwise, it stops not for illness or dismemberment or flood or fire, not for a single high holy day. And not for Dad.

Sister is winding up her be-good-during-summer homily—*Remember who you are! Remember your good character!*—but I can't take my eyes off the Oxford, after weeks of pretending it wasn't there. The world looks wrong after a death, its elements tilted, the insides of things exposed in ways you don't want to see; but you do see, you know things you don't want to know. Dad had come home every

Christmas with a complimentary turkey—a good fat one, Mum always said, not one of those poverized critters people shot in the woods. Which is the kind of thing that, after a while—whether you passed your eight hours in the blow pits or the woodyard, whether you were a timekeeper or a hydraulics man—led you to think you owned the place. That your work couldn't be underestimated. That the men in Manhattan respected you, maybe even loved you.

I'd expected the place to *drop* with the news; I thought the clouds should shrink to plumes the size of cattails. Dad loved Hugh Chisholm's mill, and that's a fact. But the men in Manhattan did not love Dad, and in the seven-almost-eight weeks since he died, the mill they owned had not skipped a single breath.

School lets out at last, the neighborhood ashriek with giddy children. My leisure hours swell with misery, just as I'd feared they would. Cathy and Betty inch back into the neighborhood, hovering at the edges of play, as I lie on the couch all day, reading anything I can find. It doesn't have to be good, or interesting, or for kids. Sister Ernestine had advised us all, as we cleaned out our desks on the last day, to continue "exploring" through the summer. You didn't have to have a car, or a destination, or someone to drive you there. No, indeed. You could roam the entire world, in any century, without so much as a bus ticket. The only thing you needed was a good book.

The first grown-up thing I'd ever read was Dad's obituary. We got two daily papers in Mexico, both published in Lewiston, a shoe- and textile-manufacturing city about forty-five miles downriver. The *Lewiston Daily Sun*, which came in the morning, skipped the Irish obits; the *Lewiston Evening Journal*, which came in the afternoon, skipped the

French. So I'd had to wait until afternoon to see that it was really, really true.

Mum had clutched the paper to her breast, murmuring, "Are you sure?" Did she think the printed words would scare me? I nodded yes, yes, and she gave in—a vibrant, etched moment in which I felt like a grown-up girl. Dad's name, ALBERT WOOD, would swell in memory to a four-inch banner—a dramatic proclamation to all of western Maine, possibly all of the United States—but in fact his stingy little notice appeared at the bottom of the page in small type, the short length and incalculable breadth of his life committed to about one column inch.

> MEXICO—Albert Wood, 57, died unexpectedly Thursday morning while preparing for work.

I liked the funnies and had never seen an obit. Other names were listed there, not just Dad's. Other families across a dozen towns had woken up on April 25, 1963, to learn what we'd learned about somebody they had loved just as much. I read it once, Cathy reading over my shoulder, our faces heating up.

"Mumma, they spelled your name wrong."

"I know."

"DOES IT SAY ABOUT DAD? READ ABOUT DAD."

Betty wanted us to read to her.

I didn't want to.

Cathy didn't want to.

So Anne read the newspaper words to Betty, her voice catching over *unexpectedly*, a gross and wounding understatement. The obituary would also appear in the *Rumford Falls Times*, our local weekly, in a version that would spell

Mum's name right. It was this version that I filched from a little stack Mum had cut out to send to relatives.

I'd read the clipping a hundred times over the past eight weeks, in secret, looking up the words I didn't know (*celebrant; communicant*) puzzling out possible tricks. Maybe there was a code somewhere. Maybe if I read the words backwards, or cut them in half and attached them back-to, they could begin to mean something else.

That issue of the *Times* had also run an ad for the Impacts, accompanied by a photo of my brother with his bandmates in their matching jackets:

Dance to the music of
THE SENSATIONAL IMPACTS
Now at the Rumford Eagles
Each Thurs and Fri
for
your dancing pleasure

These two items, opposite news in every possible way, converged as a quiet gnawing in my gut. I took a fervid interest in the *Times* after that—there was so much to know! All those obituaries, and people still went dancing. Frowning through the headlines and sidebars, I looked up words and read about the other people in my town. Every so often I'd find more news of us, either another ad for the Impacts, or an item from the high school (*At the school assembly, Miss Anne Wood gave out the English award*).

And so, after Sister Ernestine releases us for the summer with her warnings and admonitions, the first place I "travel" to is those inky pages, reading everything I can manage, including all the obits, where I discover the same two words over and over: People die either *unexpectedly* or after *lingering*. Fast or slow, take your pick. I read with a kind of curious terror, learning that words can pin their readers to place, confer permanence on the ethereal, make the unimaginable true.

The *Times* comes only once a week, and there isn't that much else in the house to read. We own a copy of *Little Women*, which I've already read twice; and the Golden Books that Father Bob buys for twenty-five cents at Sampson's—easy and colorful and way too young for me now. The other books belong to Anne, small-print books with vaguely risqué covers showing people either emerging from or entering into shadow. *Jude the Obscure*, which I assume to be a book about the crucifixion of Our Lord Jesus Christ, sports a messy ink drawing of an unhappy foreign fulla in a formless garment. Judas, I figure, post-betrayal.

The other covers are equally daunting, Victorian women and rapacious-looking men lounging beneath confounding titles like *Daniel Deronda* or *Tess of the d'Urbervilles*, or soulless covers with fat blue typeface—*Journeys into British Literature*—with no pictures at all. I consider the Mexico Public Library, whose bookshelves I know by heart, but like Mum I've developed a dread of public places. So I stay home, reading what I already have, determined to explore through literature, as Sister Ernestine said we should.

In the absence of other choices, I reread *Little Women*, a book stuffed with Victorian locutions I have to look up again. Four girls, father off to war—the story opens in me like a wound, the March family's troubles nearly unbearable this time around. Meg, the oldest, would be Anne: sensible, wise, benevolent. Like most girls I imagine myself in the role of Jo, tough and bright and living by the pen. Cathy would be Amy, the impulsive one; and Betty, of course, would be

Beth: the frail daughter, the lighted soul, the innocent at the core.

I'd always loved books for their reassuring heft, for their promise of new words, for their air of mystery, for the characters who lived in them, for the sublime pleasure of disappearing. But not until now, at the threshold of this perilous summer, have I ever turned to storybooks for instruction. Might we be the Marches, crossed by fate but headed for redemption? Like them, might we be rewarded for bearing up? Mr. March comes home at the end of the story, a miracle I know my family can't have, though I pray for it anyway.

Mum gives me her old, overloved copy of *Anne of Green Gables*, a second printing from 1906 passed along from her own mother. In miserable shape, my heirloom has a half-glued binding and defacements committed by my younger, preliterate, pencil-wielding self. Perhaps Mum thinks I'll take comfort in a fictional redheaded orphan who lives in Dad's homeland, that precious place I've never seen. Anne of Green Gables's foster mother is strict and watchful, just like Mum; her foster father, Matthew Cuthbert, is a big softie, just like Dad. And just like Dad, Matthew dies. Anne grieves hard, though her cracked world mends itself by the end, for she is cocky and strong and older than me and not even real, her life cushioned by a hundred thousand glittering, old-fashioned words from a lady author whose typing fingers can be trusted to write a happy ending. Down here in the lengthening daylight of Mexico, Maine, I'm stuck in the masculine hands of God, who, as far as I can tell, is a mean and careless writer, a ham-fisted hack, a lumbering, tone-deaf pretender.

Then I meet Nancy.

I find her one flight down, in the Hickeys' apartment, which contains many seductions — bone-white dinner plates with gold trim; a spice rack filled with colorful powders; stuffed chairs unmolested by cats—but none so dazzling as Norma's frilly bedroom, the same footprint as ours exactly, tenanted by only one adult rather than one adult and three children. Shelved in Norma's tall, white, snow-clean bookcase are twenty volumes of the *Nancy Drew* mystery series, their numbered spines facing out, arranged in order, alluringly logical.

Nothing these days has order, or logic—but look at this.

"You want to read one?" Norma asks, reaching over my head—she's tall and big-boned, a twenty-two-year-old woman, Anne's old high-school chum who, like Anne, loves kids. She plucks volume 1 and hands it over: *The Secret of the Old Clock* by Carolyn Keene, the cover art presenting Nancy, a beautiful teenager, wearing a snappy little number from the forties, a modest but form-fitting blue dress that doesn't hamper her serious work of prying open a clock face with a screwdriver. On the gladed ground, her trusty flashlight; behind her, a dark, billowing sky. Though the paper in this book feels cheap and middling—not Oxford paper, not at all—I open it to the middle, stick my face in deep, and inhale. That's Dad.

The story follows a foolproof formula that I'll get to know well in the coming days. Old Nance is a fearless girl, lousy with pluck, who can tie knots and decipher codes and shadow Suspicious Characters and read handwriting upside down. I will come to understand that my home-cut hair is not embarrassingly "red" like Dad's, but rather a comely and unpronounceable hue called "titian." Nancy has a useless boyfriend and two loyal girl sidekicks and her own room and her own car. She has no mother—a horror I can't begin to fathom. The Drews' housekeeper, a plump, pie-making cliché named Hannah Gruen, fills the bill just fine. Nancy

72

does have a father (does she ever): Carson Drew, a dashing lawyer who gladly suffers Nancy's meddling and never raises his voice (*I am sorry that my confidence in you was a little shaken, Nancy dear*), even after her near-miss from a burglar's tire iron or a scuffle with Suspicious Characters on a steeply pitched rooftop. Though I make a halfhearted stab at pretending we're the Drews, the formula doesn't fit any better than that of the Marches or the Cuthberts. Nancy has no sibs, for starters, and if she misses her absent parent she makes no sign.

Even if my family does not remotely resemble the Drews—a reality I perceive before the first cliffhanger of the first chapter of the first volume—might it still be possible for me (individually, personally, me alone) to resemble Nancy? Isn't titian hair a fair start? I tap on our walls in search of secret passages, inspect crumples of paper for tossed-away codes. Every day, sometimes twice, I knock on Norma's door to return the book I've read and borrow the next in the series, my own personal lending library. I cannot believe my good fortune, and I all but *eat* those fearful-grand books, each one opening onto the same sensational landscape, twenty-five chapters each, where nothing worse than a conk on the head is allowed to happen to anyone, including the villains.

I live inside Carolyn Keene's *oeuvre* all day while the sun shines pitilessly on our neighborhood, while Cathy and Betty sleepwalk from yard to yard, playing Red Rover at the Gagnons' or climbing on the swings at the Gallants' or ogling the pigeon coop at the Fourniers', who keep twenty tame birds, all the humdrum pastimes that, for us, have been drained of color.

"Enough," Mum warns, snapping a *Nancy* from my clutches. "You haven't been outside in five days."

She, on the other hand, hasn't been outside for nine-going-on-ten weeks, if you don't count Sunday Mass and two trips to the bank. Nobody drives, so we've been getting groceries a few at a time; Father Bob brings a tin of coffee or store-bought cookies once a week. Her eyes shine in quiet desperation behind her blue-frame glasses. "You need air," she says, more gently. "A little sunshine on your face."

Eventually I trudge downstairs with *The Secret of Shadow Ranch* (volume 5) or *The Message in the Hollow Oak* (volume 12) or *The Clue of the Tapping Heels* (volume 16) to find a tree to read beneath, reading more and more slowly, trying to make them last. As June melts into July, I start again with volume 1. I crave Nancy's matching clothes and her blue roadster and her preternatural ability to know a clue when she sees one. Like the numbered volumes in which she appears, Nancy's mind works in a comforting, knowable order. She *deduces*. She always gets the right answer.

"What are you reading?"

I look up. It's Denise, standing nearby with her bicycle. We were friends at school but I haven't seen her since school let out.

"Nancy Drew. She's a sleuth."

"I love Nancy Drew." Denise lays her bike on the grass, and in the miraculous way of childhood friendships, this moment—or a moment like it, small and unremarkable—marks our first as best and lifelong friends.

"You have to leave your bike outside the fence," I tell her. Our landlords are fussy about their grass, their driveway, their everything.

Denise moves her bike, then sits on the grass with me. She tilts my book to look at the cover.

"I don't have this one."

"I've already read it," I say. "I'll ask Norma if you can borrow it."

Denise looks at me for a moment; she likes me a lot, but like other children she's a little bit afraid of me because my father died. "You want to come over to my house?"

I look up; I can see her block on Brown Street from here—she, too, lives on the top floor—just over the rooftop of the O'Neills'.

"Okay."

Unbeknownst to Denise—or anyone—I've begun writing my own mystery, starring a titian-haired girl with no freckles. This character, named Nancy Drew—but not *the* Nancy Drew—will solve *The Mystery of the Missing Man.* I've cracked open a clean pack of Dad's paper, feeling a little like Ferdinand Magellan setting out in his ship. I've set goals: A man will go missing in Chapter 1. Cliffhangers will ensue. Then the man will be found. In an act of authorial benevolence, I've exhumed Nancy's mother (*Nancy, dear, you really must try harder to keep out of trouble!*) and retained her "prominent attorney" father, but I've ditched the housekeeper, the boyfriend, and the girl sidekicks. My Nancy will do her sleuthing alone.

I've written two pages full of beginning—Nancy's mother, Nancy's father, Nancy's house, Nancy's yard, Nancy's clothes and car and meals—searching, I suppose (in my book, in every book), for a family with no missing pieces, the family we used to be. When I follow Denise up the stairs of her block, where her beautiful mother and father say *Hello, Monica!*, my eyes sting open. There we are.

5

Too Much Stairs

THE VAILLANCOURTS ARE CATLESS but otherwise without flaw: mother, father, three girls, and a boy. Mr. Vaillancourt, a hydraulics man whose job is to prevent disaster, rotates through the mill's myriad departments on first shift with his tools and hardhat, looking the massive machinery up and down, thinking, *I'll fix you before you can break.* Mrs. Vaillancourt is pretty and kind and named Theresa, like our school, like my middle name, which I decide to start spelling with the French *h*.

It hurts her some to see me here, quivering at the top of her stairs, asking *Is Denise home?*, craning to see into the kitchen. She, too, lost her father young, feels it afresh every time she hears the timorous knock and opens the door and it's me.

"Would you like to call home?" Mrs. Vaillancourt asks when suppertime comes and I make no move to leave. I want to stay so badly.

77

"Please, Mum," I whisper into the Vaillancourts' receiver. What I don't say: I love it here. No cats but so what? I love this sense of order, the impossibility of catastrophe. Mr. Vaillancourt's in the *prevention* business. This seems like a place where nothing can go wrong.

"You're not being a pest?" Mum asks.

"No, Mum," I tell her. "Honest. Mrs. Vaillancourt *asked*."

"Well . . ." Mum says. She knows the Vaillancourts from church; they're good people, devout people. But in truth my mother doesn't want me at another mother's table. I ate here last night, too; will people think she's farming out her kids to keep them fed?

And there's this: She misses me.

"All right," she says. "But come home right after."

Mrs. Vaillancourt finds another chair in a kitchen no bigger than ours, adding a kid to the four already assembled, one of them so little she hasn't gotten the hang of a fork. When Mr. Vaillancourt presses us to converse in French, I feel grown-up, included in my pretend family practicing *s'il vous plaît* and *merci* and *passez le lait*, a good Catholic family unscarred by death. Despite the aprons we must wear to protect our clothes, supper here unfolds as a pleasing, chatty affair, and I even like the change in menu, most notably Mrs. Vaillancourt's "hamburg steak," flattened ground beef baked on a cookie sheet and served up in rectangles with A-1 sauce. Yum.

Then I go home—content and vaguely guilty—to hug my mother hard.

Wednesday at the Vaillancourts: hamburg steak. Thursday at the Vaillancourts: American chop suey. Friday at the Vaillancourts: fish sticks with ketchup. On Saturday Mum insists that I ask Denise up for supper.

"Can't I go there? They invited me."

"You have a home," Mum says.

"But—"

"It's polite to return favors. That's what well-brought-up children do."

First I have to walk to Fisher's to pick up something special—pork chops. We're having pork chops with applesauce. Then Mum sends me back out again, this time all the way "down the corner" to Sampson's, our first and only supermarket, because she's run out of something that's nobody's business and the clerks at Sampson's aren't as likely to know me as one of the Wood girls.

Returning home for the second time, I round the corner and—

Oh, shoot.

The Norkuses are out.

Our landlords have installed themselves at their post—the first-floor landing—whence they can surveil, like perched owls, the stairs and the driveway and the garden and the mailboxes and the trash shed. Mr. Norkus—we call him Jurgis—can be gruff and bewildering, using ambiguous hand gestures to fatten up seemingly unrelated instructions. He rarely smiles, though on occasion, through layers of language and history and foreignness, he can surprise our whole block with a joke. As in, the last time Mrs. Hickey went to the store:

Where you go?

Fisher's. Chicken's on sale.

On sale 'cause they die themself! No have to kill! HAHAHA!

His wife—we call her Mrs. Norkus—is ancient and vaguely military in bearing, her command so absolute that even when she isn't guarding the landing I know the heat of her presence. She keeps watch through wind and rain and sleet and dark of night, support hose rolled down to the tops of her Keds. Her white duck-cloth hat, which on anyone else might add a note of whimsy, reminds me of a helmet from World War I, something she probably knows a thing or two about.

The Norkuses came to America with rags on their feet. That's how Mum and Dad had always told it, an oft-repeated detail from which I assembled a larger drama: disembarkment in a cold rain, the words *Mexico, Maine*, pinned to a rotting sleeve, the thronged and misty vista of New York Harbor. They'd stumbled stiff-kneed down a gangway, impossibly young and yearning to breathe free, a sepia-toned couple impossible to connect with the Technicolor czars who swivel their joint gaze toward me as I come up the driveway with my grocery bag.

"Hi," I say. I bend to pat Tootsie, tightening my grip on the bag.

"Lazy poodie!" Jurgis yells. He means the cat, a white tumbleweed with gum-pink ears. "Lazy poodie!" he yells again, then a downpour of Lithuanian accompanied by laughter—or something—and a slashing gesture with his open palm.

Translation one: I am happy my cat pleases you. Is she not exquisite?

Translation two: I intend to chop off your head. Wait here while I prepare the cleaver.

"Uh . . ." I say. "Okay."

Sister Ernestine had skipped right over Lithuania, its war-torn history, its imports and exports, and so I'm left with no map, no assigned reading, no worksheets that might help me understand the Norkuses. Mexico brims with Franco *mémères* and Italian *nonnas* and Irish grandmas who speak in burred English, but the Norkuses alone seem like visitors from another country.

Jurgis gives the cat a perfunctory pat and tromps down the stairs toward his backyard garden, leaving me alone with Mrs. Norkus. Alone.

"What you gut, Munnie?"

I freeze like a bunny in the brush.

"Munnie! What you gut?"

"Groceries," I say, caught literally holding the bag.

Mrs. Norkus hooks the lip of the bag with one finger and peers in. *"Ash-ash, ticka-ticka, push-push."* She shakes her head.

Mum has a secret and Mrs. Norkus knows what it is.

"She looked in the *bag*?" Mum fumes, flinging the goods onto our narrow counter, the bloody shame of it for all to see: beef kidney. Packaged in cardboard and cellophane.

Red. Pricey. Bite-size.

For the cat.

In the Norkuses' world, this petty crime against the frugal-minded, food-chain-respecting citizens of the United States of America is a mortal sin of profligacy, certainly for a new widow with three little girls and a monthly Social Security check. But Mum's a fool for animals, especially cats, and most especially Tom, our muscled, odoriferous, anvil-headed tabby who sits on the sewing machine all day staring into the birdcage. We have other cats, but Tom is Mum's loverman now, her gentleman caller, her heater in the bed, and she'll do anything to make him happy, upgrading his chow in unwitting increments until he's eating exotic cuts we have to ask for special.

The Norkuses, on the other hand, eat from the land. Even now, so early in the summer, their vegetable garden has thickened with frilly rows of carrots and beets, its perimeter trimmed with lacy stalks of dill, pumpkin-colored marigolds, and dark fronds of rhubarb. They separate this bounty from the yard (*No go in garden!*) with a gated wire fence lined with viburnums we call the snowball bushes. As Mum rages in the kitchen—"She looked in the *bag!*"—mortified at being exposed as a spendthrift, I steal out to our back porch and look down.

Jurgis is bent over, harvesting greens from the lettuce bed and weeding between clumps by hand. At the garden's northeast corner, just over the back fence, flourishes a second garden, equal in breadth, the one tilled by Margie's nana, Jurgis's sister. Like Jurgis, Margie's nana is out there, too, slow-moving between the beanpoles in her swishing cottons. The siblings do not speak, or wave, or even face each other over the stone's throw that separates them. Nana and Jurgis's only sign of kinship survives in their rainbow of vegetables, a paean to the motherland. They live close enough to call *I sveikata!* if one of them sneezes, but they've been hardened by family trespasses too fossilized to undo. Instead of forgiveness, they cultivate cabbages big as bowling balls, purple-black beets that dye your fingers pink, squashes the color of sunshine; and they harvest their prizes alone.

Such a mystery, these siblings who came through untold heartbreak to get here. In the wake of my own heartbreak I'd watched them prepare their plots back in May, the ground still tough and cold and marred by dirty blots of snow; they'd dug and dug, undaunted. And now, green things gush from the ground. Crouching behind the porch rail, I watch Jurgis nursing his garden, Nana nursing hers, these old, Lithuanian-speaking mysteries who grow such luscious things. Haunted by their slow motion, their bent backs, their profound silence, I feel in my own heart a bloom of pain, then rush back inside to my own broken family.

"The *nerve!*" Mum is saying, slapping pork chops into the

electric frying pan. Little things knock her clean off her axis now. "The *nerve* of that woman!"

"Here," Anne murmurs. "Let me." It's actually too early to start supper—time slips around for Mum these days—so my sister turns off the pan, removes the chops, sets them on wax paper to salt and pepper them. Mum forgot.

She sits down hard. Why is she so angry? "I'd like to give them a piece of my mind," she says. But she can't. She's afraid of being *evicted*—a new word since *deceased*, a word that can halt our *yes you did no you didn't* bickering in mid-shriek ("Are you two looking to get us *evicted*?")—a word even more sinister than *strike*.

"Can I go get Denise now?" I ask.

"Go ahead," Mum says, composing herself. She's still fuming but doesn't want us to know.

I get there moments too late to watch Mr. Vaillancourt unpack his lunch pail, that coming-home ritual I love; he's been called back in, something wrong with the Number Five paper machine. I hide my little wallop of disappointment by telling Mrs. Vaillancourt that we're having pork chops special for Denise. Over here they're having meat loaf, which I hate but would eat anyway.

"Make sure to say thank you," Mrs. Vaillancourt reminds Denise as we head out. "'Thank you very much' is what you say." We walk from her block to mine, around the mailbox and down Gleason Street and then Worthley Avenue and then—

Oh, shoot.

The Norkuses are back at their post, settled into chairs. Jurgis is reading the *Times*; Mrs. Norkus isn't. "*Ash-ash*," she murmurs to her husband.

"Just act normal," I tell my friend.

"What—?"

"Shh. Do what I do."

We saunter up the driveway. We make a move for the stairs.

Jurgis lowers his newspaper with a menacing crackle. "No bring friend!" he growls. "Too much stairs!"

A squeak of shock from Denise, who rabbits back into the driveway and gapes at me, aghast. Now what? I look up, my mother so near and yet so far. Feigning indifference, I trudge over to my friend, my consolation, my supper guest, and whisper, "Pretend we're going back to your house." We stroll away, then run the whole block in the opposite direction, ending up on the blind side of the house where even the Norkuses, who have more eyes than a fly, can't spot us. From here, we hatch a multistage plan for smuggling Denise past the border guards, splitting up like soldiers on a recon mission.

We'd been unwittingly preparing for this task, roaming the neighborhood as "girl sleuths"; we'd written in our notebooks and hidden behind trees; we'd followed footprints that led nowhere, searched low branches for ominous scraps of cloth, trailed hapless souls who curdled our nerve with the first dirty look. We'd written a code that coordinated with the movement of curtains across our respective top-floor windows, a lexicon of phrases that I'd churlishly kept from Cathy, who threatened to invent a competing code but didn't, as I'd predicted, have the juice to write it all down.

Now Denise and I prepare for a fully executed stakeout. She makes a dash around back and dives behind the snowball bushes to hide; I continue up the driveway, plunk myself on the front steps, and pretend to bask in the late-afternoon daylight.

Mrs. Norkus has gone inside, probably to cook supper,

but Jurgis is still here, eyeing me over the top edge of the paper. "Where's Tootsie?" I ask him, hoping he'll go inside to fetch the cat, whom he adores. But he wasn't born yesterday.

I glance at the shivering snowball bush. I wait and wait—even the Norkuses have to pee on occasion—but nothing happens until Mrs. Norkus calls Jurgis in for supper. He folds up his paper, eyes me again, and as soon as he turns his back I shriek, "Now!," whereupon Denise springs from the green like a flushed quail.

"*Ash-ash ticka-ticka!*" Jurgis shouts. "No bring friend! Too much stairs! Make stop you jump!" Mrs. Norkus, too, has suddenly materialized, towering and foursquare. Instead of breaking for the stairs, as I do, Denise recoils in terror.

Please don't go! I think. *They're harmless!* More than anything, I want Mum to get her wish for me to look like a well-brought-up returner of favors.

I'm at the top of the first flight, but Denise is down there in the yard, her mouth forming a little *oh* of horror, so I trudge earthward and join her, the Norkuses faintly *push-push*ing in Lithuanian.

Denise regards me with something akin to awe. "Maybe . . ." I say to her. *Think! Think!* But I've got nothing.

Then, a dainty tread on the stairs above us, and Anne appears. Bermuda shorts, crisp white blouse, hair done up in a chignon: the pretty schoolteacher on summer break. She smiles at the Norkuses, who nod in turn. "Suppertime," she says, and we follow like found lambs, away from the thwarted Norkuses and toward Mum's pork chops and baked potato and cherry pie. All of it smells so good. Anne and Mum exchange a look. Mum pulls out a chair for my friend.

"Come on in!" I say, with a theatrical sweep of the arm. Welcome! Here is our laden table, our full cupboards, my mother spooning out applesauce and my sisters waiting at the table. A family at supper. Everything, to all appearances, still whole.

Norkus Rules:
NO GO IN GARDEN!
NO CAR IN DRIVEWAY!
NO TOO MUCH GARBAGE!
NO BRING FRIEND!
NO PUT BIKE ON GRASS!
MAKE STOP YOU JUMP!
TOO MUCH STAIRS!

For a long time I thought these rules, like the God of my childhood catechism, had always been and always would be. But a singular, lucid memory points a different way. It unfolds in the garden—their forbidden garden—during our time of bounty.

"Dad," I said. "Daddy?"

I was lying next to him on the grass, fearful of an ant navigating the hairy, complicated whorls of his ear.

"There's a ant in your ear, Dad. Daddy? There's a ant in your ear."

He was half asleep, on his back, his shirt soft and plaid. We'd been picnicking. Hot and sweaty, I'd swooned down next to him, out of breath, which means we girls must have been running among the Norkuses' early plantings of corn and cukes and pole beans. We'd been let loose among the stakes and twine and the Popsicle sticks that marked fragile rows of parsnips and beets.

Where does this memory come from? Mum is there, and we three girls. Anne is away—at college, I presume—so I could be as young as five.

"Dad? Daddy?"

"He'll find his way out," Dad said of the ant that had so captured my concern; he grinned, eyes closed. So I relaxed. Dad said the ant was all right and so it was.

"Dad? Do ants go to heaven?"

Oh, how did he answer? If only I could dredge his voice back through the murk of time, to know his thoughts on this, on everything. The garden memory, like all memory of Dad, lives as a shard of mica embedded in smooth gray stone. This lovely man, irretrievable but through these glints and flickers. So I recall, or imagine that I recall, how the sun beat down on my reddened, snoresome father, how I admired the male, sandpaper stubble along his jaw, his solid chest, the fact that he was unafraid that an ant might get inside him. But ever more astounding, as this memory unspools, is that we are lounging *inside the garden* and no Norkus appears to order us out.

This trespass is so electrifyingly against the rules that it could not possibly—not then—have been the rules.

And this memory: a shopping trip on a Saturday morning, Dad packing us into the car for a trip to Congress Street, the heart of Rumford's business district. We were going to buy shoes. *Sensible* ones, Mum had warned him, unnecessarily. All the kid sections in all the shoe stores in all of Rumford displayed sensible shoes and nothing but—a monochrome of boring, boyish, tie-up shoes worn by all of Mexico's schoolchildren, shoes built to last from September to June. We didn't complain; why would we? No child we knew wore stylish shoes. We were all too "heedless" for trim and rivets and patent leather, too "hard" on our things.

We followed Dad into Lamey's to look things over. Cathy wasn't feeling quite right, pale and belly-achy, so she took the first ones she spotted, a bland and stolid pair that fell nimbly within Mum's exacting guidelines. Cathy was still little, not yet in school, not yet in the habit of questioning logic, rules, nuns, the very turning of the earth. So she'd picked her pair without a fuss. Betty picked what Cathy picked, and I would have, too, had I not been thunderbolted by a pair of red shoes in the store window, an apparition—from Oz, it seemed; from Dorothy herself—magically dropped into a dowdy sea of shoes more suited to the Wicked Witch's flying monkeys.

"Can I try them, Daddy?" I pleaded, all but undone with desire.

"They're a rig," he said. Which meant he liked them.

A man with pretty eyelashes cradled my foot and eased it into the handsomest shoe I'd ever known or thought to imagine. I pointed my toe. I turned my ankle, fetchingly this way, fetchingly that way. I tried the other one. My feet in these ruby slippers were beautiful. My whole self—beautiful. Dorothy was a Kansas clodhopper compared to me.

"Please, Dad?" I asked. So he bought them.

Mr. Eyelashes rang us up. Three boxes and only one of them glowed. "Isn't your grampy nice to buy you these shoes," he said.

We bristled like insulted cats as our too-old father laughed—a loud, chortling hee-haw—then carried the tale home to Mum, who also found this outrage hootingly funny. Good thing, too; when Dad unveiled the shoes, she said, *For crying out gently* (which meant *Oh, all right*), still snickering over having married a grampy.

My shoes had a natty little ankle strap, and pinkish cross-stitching along the toe end, a ludicrous extra. In the slat of sunlight coming through the kitchen window, the leather took a vigorous shine, its red the dark, dressy hue of a freshly laid brick.

Why did these shoes mean so much to me? Dad had

given me my name (*Why don't we call her Monica?* he said to my groggy mother, who was too surprised to say no), but this new gift from him unfurled as a conscious pact, a mutual inkling that miracles lay dormant everywhere, that one could navigate the world as an optimist and be rewarded for it.

Tock, tock, tock went my red shoes on the stairs. Every tap of their heels pleased me. *Tock, tock, tock* on too much stairs. Which meant the rules must have been different before. Or, that the rules were the same but didn't quite signify when we had a man in the house.

Suddenly I see Dad's car—not the Chrysler but the one before that, a bulbous Pontiac in a shade of green I still love, parked in the driveway where cars are not allowed. And I see the new car, too, gleaming on the swept asphalt. I see our garbage tossed into the trash shed uninspected. I see bags and bags of groceries floating unmolested past the first-floor landing. I hear Dad's steadfast tread. *If those aren't the most desperate-foolish rules,* say the footfalls of a man with a thundering laugh, a man with Popeye forearms, a man who works sixteen hours at a crack and holds tabby cats cradle-style. Make all the rules you want, fulla; they don't apply to me.

Because Denise insists that I walk her downstairs after our special pork-chop supper, Mum gives me the rent money—"As long as you're going." Dad had always paid the rent himself, but now, on Saturday nights, Cathy and I draw straws; the loser has to creep downstairs with seven dollars and hand it over in the cabbage-y smog of the Norkus kitchen. That's our chore. Our contribution to the running of our fragile household.

Tonight the job is mine because I've had the honor of

hosting a friend. Denise creeps down the stairs ahead of me, peering around each landing. "They don't yell on the way down," I assure her, but she can't be convinced. On the bottom landing no Norkuses appear, but Denise sneaks past on her toes anyway. As she hits the driveway and makes her dash for home, I heave a great sigh—the kind of noise you might hear at a guillotine—and knock on the Norkuses' door.

"Thank you, Munnie," says Mrs. Norkus as I thrust the bills into her hand.

Everything down here in cabbageland emanates Old World mystery, vaguely Communist, even as we transact the American capitalist exchange of money for shelter. "Seven dulla," Mrs. Norkus whispers, filling out the receipt. I wait, wordless. She says nothing of the NO BRING FRIEND infraction from earlier. For all their bluster, the Norkuses' anger doesn't accumulate; they keep starting over from scratch.

"Seven dulla, seven dulla." Her handwriting, like everything else I associate with her, is deliberate, effortful, correct. She gives me the receipt. "You wait." She opens a box, lifts out a chocolate. "You take," she says. I hold out my hand as ordered. Mrs. Norkus places the droplet in my palm, whereupon I thank her as I've been taught, stuff the chocolate into my mouth, and make a break for the door.

When I get back upstairs, Anne's washing Betty's hair and Cathy's in the parlor watching the *Jackie Gleason Show*. Mum is nowhere, with Tom purring in her arms, nowhere. She looks at me and comes to. She smiles. "What a good eater." She means Denise, who cleaned her plate as her mother had warned her to.

"It was so good, Mum. She liked it."

"Do you get pork chops over there?"

I shake my head no, even though she knows this already.

"Mum?" A pause. "Mumma?"

She looks at me.

"Why do we live in a block?"

This question has never occurred to me until now. After the day's Norkus drama, seeing Mum staring at nothing in a kitchen that costs seven dollars, I wonder: Why wouldn't Mum want her own kitchen, her own window boxes, her own trash cans, her own stairs on which her kids can run wild?

So she tells me a story—not all of it on this particular night; not all of it in any case—but some of it. Enough. All her life, she believed in God. She believed in Jesus and Mary and Joseph and St. Anthony and the pope and the president. But she also believed, shyly, in her own turbulent intuitions. One of these intuitions, rooted in a dream, was that if she and Dad bought a house, something bad would happen to him. This warning had lived in her, undimmed through all their years in the Norkus block, until Dad came home from work, a year before he died, with three words: *Contract. Overwhelmingly. Approved.*

Overwhelmingly, Dad said. And why not? The Oxford at peak production then, the town's population growing, the schools so bloated with fourth-graders that both Rumford and Mexico had plans to build a new high school.

Mum said, *Maybe it's time.*

She didn't have to ask Dad twice. He longed for his own garden to replace his backyard patch at Aunt Rose and Cumpy's. He wanted his own soil. His own fence. His own claim on a quarter acre of sunshine.

They didn't look far—Mum didn't want to move far—and the right house did not appear. Then, in February, two months before Dad died, snow still banked over the Norkuses' petunia planters, Mum got wind of a house up the street that had been sold without a FOR SALE sign. The Desjardins place: single-family, two stories, big yard, corner lot.

"It would have been perfect," Mum says. "I couldn't believe that house was gone. On the market a month and I never heard a word." She puts down the cat, shakes her head. "I was just sick about it. Sold right under my nose."

Her crushing regret, however, had turned out to be a blessing in disguise—didn't everything?—for shortly after losing out on the Desjardins place, she dreamed Dad's death. Dreamed that her fifty-seven-year-old husband dropped dead on his way to work.

Then she dreamed it again. And once more. Then it happened.

For nearly three decades she'd declined to buy a house in case something bad befell him—a mill accident her most reasonable guess—and just when she thought it safe to succumb to her heart's desire, her fear came true.

"Imagine if we'd bought it," she says, her arms twining me now. She's still mad at Mrs. Norkus for peering into the grocery bag; but she's also glad to have given my friend a classy meal as recompense, and glad to have a place to live, a place she knows, and she's a little sorry to have gone all balled up over something as silly as beef kidney. She's "offered it up"—to God, who apparently has some secret use for her troubles. "Can you imagine," she murmurs, "a big house like that to manage all by ourselves? Think of the mortgage to pay, storm windows to put up, a boiler on the fritz."

What I think: my own room, with two windows.

"Oh, it haunts me," she says, shuddering. "That near-miss." She's speaking of God's benevolence, the hand of the Father guiding those other people to the Desjardins place, preventing the soon-to-be widow from getting in too deep.

"It's a miracle I didn't hear about it," she whispers. "We'd have bought it for sure." I linger in her embrace, as she adds, "God provides, Monnie. We don't always see it until after."

It does not occur to her, and certainly not to me, that had she and Dad bought a house at the beginning, we'd have a paid roof over our heads. Instead, as I'm washing my face before bed, I glance out the bathroom window, which looks directly up the street to the Desjardins place. The yard is full of toys. "Move," Cathy says, elbowing past me to get a towel. "Move *yourself*," I tell her. *That's mine no it isn't yes it is.* Believing we've been touched by miracle, I stare at the large lighted windows of our averted calamity, thinking: *Thank God thank God thank God.*

The Norkuses, of course, had sorrows of their own. "No see my mamma again," Mrs. Norkus had told Mum one day, when asked about her family back in Lithuania. The Norkuses let down their guard sometimes, punctuated their soldiering fortitude with glints of kindness. I feared their mossy English, their owlish stares, their curtains that looked spun by giant spiders, but it was Jurgis, it is said, who'd asked to hold the newborn me on my first day home. When I was three I'd named Mum's parakeet Jurgis, apparently detecting something in our landlord that was feathery and soft and aching to communicate. The Norkuses gave us squash and tomatoes from the forbidden garden; they'd once invited us to their camp at Roxbury Pond, urging us to glory in the view, the water, the new spindles on the porch rail. *More swim in pond!* they'd called. *More eat hamburg!* We'd come back baffled and sunburned, Dad chuckling at the wheel, our trunk stuffed with freshly cut flowers.

What had they thought of Dad? Had they seen him as a fellow traveler who'd abandoned a bucolic, beloved, but dead-end homeland to embrace an industrial rebirth? Or did they view his journey, a brief ferry ride and then a train to prosperity and happiness, as the voyage of a pretender, a man who had it too easy? Is it possible they were cowed by Dad's painless passage, the way he slipped into town already speaking the language, so comfortable in his skin?

The Norkuses, who missed nothing, surely heard Cathy tromping down the stairs on the day Dad died. They saw her pass the landing in her school uniform. Watched her trudge down the driveway and head toward school. What did they think of this? There was so much of America they didn't understand; every Halloween they'd stare at us with pained and baffled faces, then pelt us with nickels before slamming the door. Was this—this child headed off to school a half-hour after her father is discovered dead twenty yards away—another indecipherable American tradition they had failed to accommodate?

The Norkuses never said of Dad, "so young, oh so young." They'd gone quiet over the news, and chastened. Mrs. Norkus probably sent up some *blynys*. They'd liked Dad; who didn't? But to the Norkuses our tragedy must have seemed ordinary enough. Fifty-seven years: not a long life, but not a short one, either. A gentle sorrow, in the grander scheme of sorrow.

How easily Dad had acquired what he wanted: work, spouse, children. The Norkuses, too, had acquired these things (though their children were now grown and gone), but unlike Dad—who came here healthy and well shod —they'd left so much more behind, their past gone for good. The Norkuses picked through our stuff and tossed almost nothing themselves, for they looked upon the trash shed as a repository for second chances.

We need our things. We protect our things. We make

rules around them if we have to. The Norkuses guarded their stairs because they loved their stairs. They had bought those stairs, and the building attached to them, by leaving their mammas and their cherry trees and their big blue sky and their language and their nation. They guarded their garden because they loved their garden. Every carrot and parsnip and rhubarb stem. They guarded their driveway because they loved their driveway. Every crack and fissure and shiny knot of frost-heaved tar.

It took years for me to know this, to see how loss can tighten your grip on the things still possible to hold.

6

Paper

THE NORKUSES HAD THEIR petunia planters, their trash shed, their garden, their stairs. What I had was paper. Oxford paper. Exquisite paper, blindingly white. Heavy enough that I knew I held a prideful product, not so heavy that it seemed too good to use. Sleek to the touch, but not too sleek. Oxford paper took the weight of a pencil with just the right give, and even the leakiest ink flowed upon it without smudging.

This is what I had, though I did not think to guard it. We ran short of sugar sometimes, or milk, or bird gravel, or shampoo. But no household in our town ever ran short of paper.

On paper day, the last Thursday of every month, Dad would come home at five-thirty—after a shift and a quarter, his foreman's hours. His clothes would be dampish, his boots sawdusty, his hands scraped and hard-callused, but he smelled like soap, for he'd taken a shower before coming home. A shower! I don't know what we girls imagined—we'd never seen a shower in person—but, my goodness, a *shower*. How filthy he must have gotten, day after day, to require one before facing Mum in her clean housedress, her hands scented with Jergens almond-cherry cream.

"Here he comes," Mum would say, hearing him on the stairs. "Go!"

Me first me first me first! We charged him like a flock of crows, pillaging his pockets for candy.

"Hey, hey, hold your horses," he laughed, which is how we remembered it was paper day.

One-two-three we stepped away and saw that under one arm was tucked his lunch pail and a bag of groceries from Fisher's; under the other, a glowing packet of paper, a thing of creaseless beauty, the clean, high-style product of Dad's grubby, overheated work. He brought it in, placed it on the kitchen table.

Dad made that.

Oh, that gorgeous, spotless stuff. It was, simply, beautiful. Though it seemed a shame to tear open the pack and dig in—we had plenty extra in the cupboard—dig in we did, working through a whole ream every few weeks.

Cathy and I drew pictures: nuns and angels; God the Father; God the Son; God the Holy Ghost with his flappy, histrionic wings. We drew cats and parakeets and neighbor dogs in idealized amity, holding hands, paw to wing. We drew ourselves, and Mum and Dad, and Anne in her pretty clothes. We drew Father Bob in his cassock, Barry playing his May Belle. We drew Cumpy with his ever-present pipe; and Aunt Rose, who worked at the Credit Union, with her jangling keys and cigarettes and new car. We drew our neighborhood, all the houses and flat-topped blocks, the neighbors and their swing sets and their porch chairs. We drew the mill, too: the stacks and conveyors and brick walls and smoky windows and the colorful hills beyond. We drew our world, over and over and over, and other worlds, too, filled with horses and sunsets and princes and castles and ladies with high hair and capacious, sky-pink ball gowns.

Betty drew snowmen.

Three circles, and a straight-line mouth that sliced the snowman's face in half and jutted past both sides. Then buttons, huge buttons almost as big as the original circles. First it didn't bother us, then it did.

"Draw something else, Bet."

"OKAY."

"That's a snowman. Draw a house, Bet. Like this."

"LIKE THIS."

"That's another snowman. What are those things?"

"BUTTONS."

"Make them like this, Bet. See? Buttons are small."

"LIKE THIS."

"That's the same thing you just drew."

"NO IT ISN'T."

"Yes it is. Another exact-same snowman with a line mouth and exact-same buttons. It looks like a little snowman inside a big snowman."

"NO IT DOESN'T." Her voice was loud but forbearing. She never once got mad at us. She suffered our corrections as if we were a song on the radio she didn't exactly enjoy but deemed not quite bothersome enough to turn off.

"Draw a house, Bet. Look, it's easy."

"Please, Bet? Pleeeeease?"

"Pleasepleaseplease draw a house."

But she didn't draw houses. Or God or princesses or trees or cats. She drew dozens of snowmen. Hundreds. Thousands.

Now that's some fearful-grand snowman, Dad said.

Three toppling circles with more circles inside. Over and over. For years she did this. And why not? We had paper to spare, and more where that came from. Our parents allotted us one pair of shoes and bathed us all three in the same lukewarm water, but when it came to paper we were allowed to be immoderate, shameless wastrels. We used one side. We started over. Flip, flip, flip went the pages, the elegant product of the beast across the river that pumped and pumped as we drew and drew and tossed the pages away and away because paper would come to us, like the sanctifying grace of God, free and forever.

The blinding-white paper was one kind; there were others, many others, with fetching names like Mainefold Enamel and Oxford Bright. Our paper got shipped all over the world, some of it in packaged sheets, some in rolls higher and wider than our parlor on Worthley Avenue. It left town in trucks and freight cars every day by the hundreds of tons, then reappeared in the world as the pages of a fourth-grade spelling book, or the label on a soup can, or an issue of a financial journal that presaged a coming decline in American manufacturing that nobody—not here, not now, the Oxford's machines at full roar—could fathom. The shoemakers, yes: a closing here or there, another rumored, piecework up and down. That's shoes for you. But not paper.

We are the Oxford! The mighty, mighty Oxford! Paper wasn't something you walked on. It was something you held.

You make paper like this: tree to log, log to chips, chips to pulp, pulp to paper. A noisy, lengthy, oversize, stinking, seemingly chaotic process that requires exaction and attention and affinity. When Dad first arrived at the mill gates as a young man, the process was already impressively mechanized, but you needed men, many men, to run and maintain the god-size machinery, to lift and load and feed and receive, to tinker eternally with a hard-used infrastructure lousy with asbestos and lead paint. You needed aptitude. You needed focus. And at some stages, you needed a certain . . . flair.

Dad came to Maine via the Canadian Pacific Railway in the fall of 1926, twenty years old and aching to earn, and moved in with his doting oldest sister, who'd set up with her husband in a block on Knox Street, a cobblestone's throw from the mill gates. He came with his boyhood friend, Jack Mooney; "P.I.'s," people called them (not kindly), with their PEI accents and PEI clothes and PEI sunburns and PEI fingernails caked with clay. Rosella packed them a lunch and they beelined over to the footbridge, showing up at daybreak in their rolled-down shirtsleeves to snap up a chance to work.

They lifted their freckled faces to the miraculous thing. They could hear churning water, either from the river below them or from something ahead, behind the brick walls.

"Big fulla," said Dad, looking up.

"Desperate large," Jack agreed. "You s'pose they'll take us?"

Dad nodded. He knew.

The odds of getting work were pretty good that year, no matter the prejudices harbored by whichever supervisor did the day's choosing. Most days, most men who wanted work got it, for a daily wage and no benefits and a chance to prove your desire. Back then you worked a twelve-hour shift with a Tower of Babel team: an Italian, a Franco, a P.I., a Lithuanian, an Irishman, a Scot. If you had no natural alliances, or a language barrier, or even a knee-jerk enmity toward your foreign-tongued crewmate, then you didn't tend to communicate beyond the requirements of running your machine. If you didn't talk, you didn't organize; if you didn't organize, you didn't get big ideas about what the mill might owe you for your work beyond your day's pay.

Dad waited, he got chosen, he entered the deafening labyrinth, where he was told where to spend the next twelve hours of his one and only life. Maybe they sent him outside, into a throbbing cold, to heft logs cut in northern Maine and New Brunswick. He ended his working life in the woodyard; maybe it started there, too.

Some of the logs back then still arrived by river, where pole men, stationed on the Androscoggin's man-made islets, poled logs marked with the Oxford blaze toward the Oxford yard and directed the rest to float on to mills downriver. Maybe Dad spent that first shift hefting logs by hand from wood piles the size of houses, loading them into the barking drums. Or he might have been directed inside to cook wood chips in sky-size rooms, filling mighty steel digesters with chips from the chip loft, or else deeper inside still, to pump cooked pulp into massive washers or bleaching vats or storage tanks, adding dyes and clays and unpronounceable chemicals to make specific pulp stock for various grades of paper.

Or maybe he worked in the beater room, beating the soupy pulp in twenty-foot tubs by raising or lowering a rotating drum, cutting and brushing the pulp fibers fine enough to make paper worth bringing home.

Or maybe they assigned him to the paper machines themselves, astounding inventions the size of battleships, their parts alive and thrumming. At the wet end of a paper machine, Dad might have filled the head box with treated pulp, or opened the slices, dam-style, to release an even stream of pulp stock onto the "wire," an immense wire-mesh screen that moved both forward and side to side, weaving the fibers and sucking out excess water, an inexorable motion that, at last, made a sheet of paper up to twenty feet wide.

Dad was a short man, though brawnily built; did he feel shrunken, beholding for the first time this mechanized breadth and height and depth? If assigned to the dry end, he might have manned the press rolls, where the sheet was snaked through massive wringers; or the dryers, where the paper passed between temperature-controlled, steam-heated cylinders—an industrial version of the hot rollers his teen-age girls would use to curl their hair long after his death. Or maybe he went to the calenders, lofty upright machines fed from the top, where the unrolling paper—now possessed of the proper color, brightness, character, and weight—undu-lated through pressurized drums made alternately of steel and felt, the soft-against-hard pressure creating a lovely burnish. If the paper had been treated with a coating, this would be the moment when it finally shone. Imagine Dad, who liked handsome things, watching this final miracle and thinking: *Now that's some desperate-handsome paper.*

Or maybe they put him on the rewinders, where the fin-ished paper got wound again, the rolls neatly sliced, like a vanilla Yule log, into varying widths. Dad may have been charged with saving the trimmed edges, which went back to the beater room to be pulped again, another chance to be-come a finished page on which a man might read the news of his adopted country, or write a lonesome letter back home to his brother and sisters standing waist deep in thistle and jewelweed, heading out to harvest the season's last tomatoes.

What was in those letters? Money, and stories: the girl he had his eye on, the dances and picture shows, the mill's munificence and mayhem. In those days, if you came to work with a flask in your pocket, if you squandered your shift glad-handing and blathering and paying half-attention, if you were slipshod in your comportment or temperament, if instead of watching roller speed you rolled your eyes at a Québécois accent or at a Lithuanian whose cabbage-*blyny* lunch offended your nose, then your distraction cost you a finger or toe, an arm or leg, or lit an explosion that turned you and the Franco and the Lithuanian and the cabbage *blyny* into a cloud of smithereens hurtling above the Androscoggin valley from the mill's churning gut.

You proved yourself by not losing your temper, not losing your focus, not losing your life. Dad proved himself quick. *Your father wasn't afraid of work*, Mum always said. After a few weeks, his first reward: a steady, six-day, twelve-hour shift in the blow pits.

Did his heart leap or sink as he entered the malodorous maw of the sulphite mill? Surely his heart leaped; work was all. But as I imagine this scene forty-five years after his death, I want to pull him back from the threshold of the life he thought he wanted, this sunny, freckled boy of twenty who carried a permanent memory of chest-high blueberry bushes and red earth. How did he enter those clanking gates after a boyhood spent beneath cloudless skies, taking in great lungfuls of fresh air tinged with the smell of new grass and old horses and the nip of the nearby sea? *Don't go in there, Dad*, I shout at his straight, long-gone back, *that work will kill you*, but of course he goes in there. He has to. He *wants* to. And if he doesn't, there's no work at all, no settling here, no Mum, no us.

So he goes in. Before Local 900. Before "air-quality index." Before mandatory safety glasses or hardhats or steel-toed boots or automatic shutoffs or safety guards or bright yellow signs telling you to tuck in your shirttail, for God's sweet sake! No OSHA no EPA no Clean Water Act. Rumford-Mexico in 1926 is an enviable axis of industry, the Oxford the largest book-paper mill in the world under one roof, a thriving moneymaker that can turn the most ordinary man into a breadwinner, a marriage prospect, a safe bet.

That was Dad, in the healthy bloom of his young manhood, sweating out his shift in the blow pits, where men young and old cooked pulp in a foul and dangerous liquor of sulphurous acid. Dad and his crewmates pressurized toxins and then released them, over and over, separating pulp from water, water from steam, steam from swill, making strong, beautiful pulp that would become strong, beautiful paper. Back then nobody troubled to collect all this poison; they saved the good stuff, flushed the rest. That was Dad's job, to open the valve and flush a toxic broth into the ancient Androscoggin River, our lifeblood river, its banks lined with ailing willows, houses disfigured with curdled paint, rooftops and windowpanes and flapping laundry blackened by pulp waste and fly ash, a deep, wide, legendary river scummed with yellow foam and burping up bloated fish as it made its eons-old pilgrimage to the sea.

As Dad filled our river with swill, Mum was sitting in civics class at Stephens High School, her hands folded on her desk behind her classmate Edmund Muskie, our future governor, senator, presidential candidate, secretary of state, and architect of the Clean Water Act. She wasn't much interested in a boy like Ed, who "always had his nose stuck in a book." Their classroom windows faced the river, and I imagine her staring out there, daydreaming about the hardier boys crossing the footbridge with their lunch pails. One of them, the one they call "Red," by now an older man of twenty-seven, will take her to a dance, and on this first official date, in an uncharacteristic burst of whimsy, he will declare to her on the jouncing wooden dance floor of the Mechanics Institute, "We'll bring up our children in the house of God!"

They did. They could. Because Dad eventually won a job as a wood scaler, a job that kept him in contact with the sky. He met trucks that came in all day long, directing the drivers to the proper wood piles after measuring the load (how high, how wide, what kind). Logs came in from Oxford-owned land in Maine and eastern Canada, but also from area farmers or woodlot owners who knew Dad for a fair deal. He must have been happy—a family man now, with a wife and a first child, his redheaded boy.

Dad scaled wood for about thirty years of shift work, until he went on salary in the mid-fifties as a foreman in the woodyard. A union man by then, he suffered a stab of regret for leaving his hourly-paid brethren. He'd now have to hire and fire, he who could not say no to a nine-year-old. But with three surprise children gracing his middle age, he had to jump at the chance.

On certain spring days the woodyard resembled brush strokes on canvas, wood gathered into glowing pyramids, their shapes shifting as sun and shadow drew out their living colors. In winter, under a pitiless midday light, the entire mill complex could appear almost fragile, its myriad shapes exposed here, snow-muffled there, its breathing presence open to the elements. In summer, at dusk, it laid bare its bones, a bleak and soulless silhouette against a dying sky. The truth behind these tableaux lay in the artless reality of industry, a pact between man and machine, management and labor. But I like to think that on certain mornings of low light, in certain seasons or turns of weather, Dad saw the mill in that other way, the mill as a living being, a bestower of pride and bounty, real as a father: benevolent, trustworthy, unfailingly present.

• • •

His shift in the woodyard usually started in the scaler's office, where he assembled the day's crews, gave the day's first orders, maybe told the day's first joke. He had crews in the yard who loaded and unloaded, and a yard crew inside, too, charged with feeding logs to the barking drum and the chipper. Outside, the wood sat in named piles. Number ten: peeled spruce. Number nine: rough hardwood, still barked. There was a pile called Bay City, named for the make of the fixed conveyor its logs would be loaded into. Dad had four, five, six crews sometimes to keep track of, new men to train, a large physical area to monitor; sometimes he drove his distances in his Pontiac (or, during his final months, in his new Chrysler) if a man had to, say, scale a delivery at the lower gate.

I imagine him as a calm-natured border collie, patiently herding all day, counting heads. When he caught a new man sneaking back over the footbridge after drinking away most of his maiden shift, Dad gave him another chance. Men got second chances, thirds. If he had a temper, we kids never saw it. When he did let someone go—even border collies have an end to their tether—he did plenty of heavy brooding. It hurt his heart to let a man go, because these years were the ones the survivors would later call the Good Old Days of the Oxford, a time when you had no desire to work anyplace else, and no reason to think you'd ever have to.

Mum wondered later whether those heedless men hastened his end; heedless men, and long hours, and poisons that found a way into his big pumping heart. Sulphur dioxide. Calcium bisulphate. Hydrogen sulphide. Methyl mercaptan. Dimethyl sulphide. "The man *lived* in that place," she often said, which meant that he'd also died in that place, bit by bit, no matter how much joy he took from the work.

The woodyard of Dad's foreman years was a shrine to automation, with cranes and loaders and conveyers moving in a mechanized dance of progress. But much of the labor was still manual and Dad didn't mind it. If a crew went short a man, Dad was the one who stepped in, shouting, "Two doors . . . one door . . . half a door . . ." at the boxcar operator lining up with the conveyor. It was Dad who might take the big hook and start scooping logs straight from the car. This was the first stage of papermaking, and Dad meant to get it right.

The assistant foreman was a hale young man they called Bunny. Bunny and Red: They were friends. Bunny worked with Dad for eight years, until that cool April morning when word came down from the gate.

It's nearly eight and Red's not in.

Red's not in? Every man within earshot knows: something deadly wrong.

They assemble in the scaler's office but nobody seems to know what to do. The supervisor, whose former job is the one Dad has now, calls around to different parts of the mill. Anyone seen Red?

Where the hell is Red?

They confer some more, as the trucks idle in the yard.

"Well, somebody should go up there. Find out what's wrong."

"Worthley Avenue. The Norkus block, right?"

"Third floor."

The supervisor sends his son, Jim, a truck foreman. If Jim came to our door I don't remember, but somebody told him something, for he's back in fifteen minutes with news.

At first nobody says anything. Then everybody at once:

"Jesus Christ. Oh, Jesus Christ."

"Just like that."

"He's got them little girls."

"His wife—"

"Oh, Christ. Somebody go tell his boy. He works in the pipers. Did somebody tell his boy?"

"I'll find out."

"How old was he? Fifty-what? Somethin' like that?"

Dad was nobody's drinking buddy, nobody's card partner, nobody's godfather or surrogate uncle or bowling-team captain. When he wasn't in the mill, he was home with us. His friendships, executed entirely inside the mill gates, spanned years, decades. They were real.

"Oh, goddammit. Goddammit. Red gone."

"I can't believe it. I gotta sit down."

"And Jack, too. Somebody tell Jack Mooney. They came here together from the Island."

"I'm gonna tell you, I can't believe it. I gotta sit down."

"Jesus Christ, don't it just make you—? Goddamn, ain't it a thing?"

"It's a thing. A fearsome goddamn thing."

But they have work to do. The trucks are lining up, the boxcar tracks hum like a summons. The conveyor makes its gimme-gimme groans. Is it worse to lose a coworker when your work involves such size, such scale, when it feeds and floats two towns?

Today is Thursday, last Thursday of the month. At day's end Dad's men will collect their paper and take it home to their own kids, who will draw upon it picture after picture of their lively, humming town.

I never thought to ask: Who replaced him? I hope it was Bunny, to whom Dad was an old reliable—twenty years older, a man who didn't dog Bunny's steps or doubt Bunny's decisions. Bunny had to get back to work that morning with everybody else; he had to stop himself a dozen times that day, squint into the sun pouring into the woodyard, and say, "I can't believe it." With contract time looming, there was a bit of unease in the air, and now this. He had to attend the wake on Friday, and then the funeral on Saturday, and then go back to work for the next twenty-five years without Red, years in which things happened to the good old Oxford that, Bunny knew, woulda broke Red's heart clean in half.

7

Three Vanillas

ONE OMINOUS NIGHT, my mystery book begins, *a titian-haired sleuth received a very ominous message.* I write in secret — top secret — on Dad's paper, heaving in with the gusto of Carolyn Keene, whom I imagine as a Jo March type: long dress, quill pen. I have no idea that in real life Carolyn Keene is a committee of work-for-hires, a literary assembly line, the writing equivalent of a paper mill.

"What are you doing?" Cathy asks.

I snatch the paper away. "Nothing." *The Mystery of the Missing Man* is mine alone, an inexplicable balm, the slow-dancing B-side to my other waking hours.

"Let me see."

"No.

"Gimme that!"

"No! It's none of your business!"

Yes it is no it isn't yes it is!

Mum calls out from our bed: "Are you two looking to get us evicted?"

We've made it through the Fourth of July. First, too many Dadless days to count; then too many weeks; now I'm counting by months. Two going on three.

I'd rather be at the Vaillancourts, where the landlords are nearly invisible and I've been thoroughly absorbed into the family routines, which are rulish but not Norkusy. No shoes indoors, dear. No food away from the table, hon. No animals in the house, please.

Mr. Vaillancourt pats my head. He looks me in the eye. He calls me dear. Mrs. Vaillancourt pats my head. She looks me in the eye. She calls me dear. They ask, *How's your mother?* They always ask, *How's your mother?*

Good, thank you. She's very good.

I don't say, *She sleeps a lot.*

I don't say, *In our bed.*

I don't say, *If Anne left I think we would die.*

I don't say, *I'm afraid my mother might be shrinking.*

I don't say, *She does everything the same but she's not here.*

I don't say, *Sometimes I pretend I live here with you.*

I don't ask Mr. and Mrs. Vaillancourt, who have brightened my days like an apology from heaven: *Why did God forget the rest of my family?*

Mum wants to know: *What's it like over there? No shoes, really? Even in summer?* It's as if with Dad gone she's lost her knack for mothering and is featuring how to get it back without having to leave home. I deliver stagy reports in the style of Dad's old PEI neighbor Mrs. McCarn, clearing our kitchen counter of bread wrappers to replicate Denise's mother's pristine kitchen, which, like ours, must be endlessly swabbed against the myriad assaults of children. Mum nods and squints, taking mental notes, intensely interested in how this other, mother-father Catholic family operates. She's grown fond of Denise, a dimpled child with large, trusting eyes and impeccable manners, to whom our household is a revelation of broken rules: cupboards unlatched, the TV on whenever we want, cats parked on tables and chairs, a talking bird lolloping from room to room and landing on mirrors and bedposts and our own heads. Mum takes in only small breaths of comfort in these suffocating weeks, and one of these comforts is Denise, who makes no secret of her wonderment.

But lately, as I head to the Vaillancourts' at afternoon shift change—the better to catch a father coming home in his dusty clothes—Mum says, *Why don't you stay here?* Softly, not sternly. *Stay here*, she says. My insides open to a flood of love and I stay.

Today it's raining anyway, a steady pelting. I fill pages and pages, working on a "setup" scene, undiscouraged. Sometimes I depart from the story to write a single word over and over, a discipline Sister Ernestine had insisted on, the better to practice our spelling and penmanship. Certain words become little obsessions, containing not only meaning and sound but an irresistible physical loveliness. I like shapely words like *coop* or *loop* or *good*, all those connected circles. In one of Anne's books I find the name *Oona*, a word I write twenty-six times: thirteen times down one side of the page, thirteen times down the other. Words like *tatter* or *letter* or *kettle* resemble forest ridges in miniature, sudden peaks of *l*'s and *t*'s jutting up from a horizon of *e*'s and *a*'s and *o*'s. Words like *ominous* or *sneer* or *simmer,* their letters all the same size, look like bridges between spiky words like *the* or *but*. What satisfaction, to know how to read, to write, to spell these words; to admire them, to pronounce them, to define them; to arrange and rearrange them; to commit them to a sheet of paper made to last.

I ravage my word collection, sifting through dozens of beauties to construct sentences, paragraphs, and, I hope, a whole, happy story for a Nancy of my making. Many of my sentences—often entire paragraphs—look remarkably like scenes written by Carolyn Keene. *"We'll just see what happens to meddling girls!!!"* *sneered the wild-eyed caretaker.* Not a single criminal in my book has regular eyes.

Nancy arrives at the home of a worried wife; Nancy speaks to a Suspicious Character; Nancy outlines the case for her "pensive" father. I fashion limitless descriptions of hats and parlors and cars and nighttime, specializing in "lengthening shadows." My time with fake Nancy is like falling into a peaceful hollow of forgetting.

But you can't write all day when you're nine-almost-ten; you can't spend every second reading the *Times*, or a *Nancy Drew* you've already read twice; you can't spend every afternoon pretending you belong to a Franco family that doesn't like cats. My idle moments swell like a beige balloon, featureless and burstable.

"You guys want to play School?" I ask my sisters.

Cathy and Betty are inside today, too; this hot July rain has lowered the whole sky, the reek of the mill nearly dizzying.

"NO," Betty says. But School is my favorite game, and Cathy's too, its rules as stringent and diverting as the real thing, so we steamroll her, as always, into the thankless role of Pupil.

Betty can't read, which has never stopped us from drilling her in the alphabet. We've taught her to print her name, to recognize a minuscule list of useful words like *God* and

Mum and *cat*. But the game is more than just fun now; we're marking off days in a summer so numbing and Dadless that it needs a word other than *summer*. It's just . . . space.

Cathy sets up the cardboard boxes; I fetch a fresh packet of Oxford paper from the cupboard.

"Good morning, children," I say. It's my turn to be the Teacher.

Cathy: "Good morning, Sister."

Betty: "GOOD MORNING, SISTER."

"Children, for today's lesson we shall read page three and page four. After that, we shall copy the words onto our sheets." I pass out two fresh leaves of Dad's paper. "Remember: Well-formed, even letters are a pleasure to the suffering eyes of Jesus." I try to look stern and martyrly, like the exhausted teachers I'm imitating. "Now, whose turn is it to read? Hmm. Betty Wood. I mean, Elizabeth Wood, in the second row. Please read page three."

"NOT ME," Betty says. "IT'S CATHY'S TURN." This is what she always says.

"Very well. Catherine Wood, in the first row. Please read page three."

"See Jane run. *Run*, Jane, *run*! Run for your *life*!"

"Excellent." It really is. Cathy spikes everything with drama and as a writer myself I don't mind the embellishments. "Now. Who's next? Hmm. Let's see. Elizabeth Wood, in the second row. Please read page four."

"RUN RUN RUN."

"No, I'm sorry, Elizabeth. That's page three."

"Let her read page three," Cathy says.

"Very well. Elizabeth Wood, please read page three."

"RUN RUN RUN."

"You're not reading. You're copying what Cathy said."

"NO I'M NOT."

"What's that word?"

"RUN."

"Is not. It's *Jane*. Catherine, please follow along with your finger to show Elizabeth the words."

"See."

"SEE."

"Jane."

"JANE."

"Run."

"RUN."

"This is stupid," Cathy gripes. "Can we do arithmetic?" Cathy considers Dick and Jane and their baby sister Sally and their unctuous parents and Spot and Puff boring goody-goodies and way too easy. But it's the only book that gives Betty a snowball's chance.

"Very well. Please turn to your Arithmetic book. Hmm. Who's next? Elizabeth Wood, in the second row. Please count for the class, starting with eight. Then we shall write the numbers on our sheets. Remember: Well-formed, even numbers are a pleasure to the suffering eyes of Jesus."

"ONE TWO THREE—"

"Starting with eight."

"ONE TWO THREE—"

"Eight-nine-*ten*," Cathy says. "Like *that*, Bet."

"EIGHT NINE TEN!"

"Excellent," I tell her. "Gold star for Elizabeth Wood. What comes after ten?"

"TEN."

Numbers are useless. There she sits at her cardboard-box desk, patiently letting me imitate—by the hour—our brilliant, exacting, autocratic nuns. We use fat red pencils still sharp from Dad's jackknife, and a wooden ruler to make lines on which a Pupil could form a jangling, uneven

B-E-T-T-Y W-O-O-D ten times if the Teacher asked. But she always gets something wrong. The tail of the *y* on the wrong side; a *b* in place of a *d*.

"That doesn't say 'Betty Wood.'"

"YES IT DOES."

"No, it doesn't."

"YES IT DOES."

"It says Batty Woob."

"NO IT DOESN'T."

I'm an excellent Teacher! I make flawless imitations of the Sisters! Why can't my Pupil write on the line? Why does my Pupil write *a* instead of *e*? Why why *why*? Her blue eyes patient and bafflingly bright, her shiny, useless ringlets cascading to her shoulders, my Pupil, whom I love with a protective, steadfast, blood-rushing ferocity, poses my second object lesson in the futility of changing a thing that is clearly the way things have to be, God's brainless plan, the bone truth.

The nuns have told Mum that Betty will go to third grade in the fall, with Cathy. Sister Mary of Jesus, the third-grade teacher, is exceedingly patient. What does Mum think of this? She steps into the parlor to end our game of School—it's time for supper, and she's just gotten up, smoothing her dress over her hips, shaking out the hem. She slips Betty's paper from our cardboard desk and examines the balloonish lettering, the backwards *y*'s. Surely she knows that third grade will be worse than second, her child stuck at a real desk for hours on end, arithmetic and grammar drills washing over her like the sound of falling water, or crows in trees, or the Oxford's sighing steam stacks. What should Mum do? Send her back or keep her home? In a few weeks she'll have to decide, but who will help her?

Anne is a schoolteacher who knows about educating; Father Bob has the ear of God; but they don't know what it feels like to be Betty's mother, or Betty's father. How hard and deeply Mum and Dad had prayed, for years, all those rosaries and novenas and midnight imprecations. After those early, faint, throat-knots of suspicion—*Come on, baby, lift your head; roll over; reach for the bunny*—and then the wing-lifts of hope—*Look, Albert; there she goes; better late than never*—and then more suspicion—*Maybe she's just a little slow*—and more hope—*Didn't I see a paper in her hand just now?*—Mum, alone now, must surrender at last to what she knows.

She rattles the sheet of Dad's paper from our make-believe school where every child gets an *A*. "Good job," she says—to Betty for writing her name and to us for teaching her. Then she gathers up our papers and adds them to the stack she keeps next to the sewing machine, missing Dad.

I slip over to the Vaillancourts' as often as I can, where Denise and I sit on the whaleback of grass that passes for her front yard, planning stakeouts or refining our code or reading Nancy's next case, Denise trying to puzzle out the plot's secrets in advance. My own secret is that I'm waiting for Mr. Vaillancourt to come home.

I wait for him.

I watch him.

I love him.

Every moment in his company feels desperate and vanishing.

"Don't tell me what happens," Denise warns me, looking up from her book. She's reading volume 9, the one where Nancy saves an orphan who turns out to be an heiress.

"Keep your eye on the guardians, that's all I'm saying."

What I've been reading in the *Times* is also a mystery.

Employees of Oxford Paper Company, goes the United Mine Workers' quarter-page ad, *you owe it to yourself and your future to obtain the GUARANTEES IN WRITING from the UPP officials . . . Watch the UPP SQUIRM AND TWIST when you demand in WRITING, guarantees to ensure your FUTURE.*

This sounds like the dramatic talk of Suspicious Characters, so I ask Mr. Vaillancourt what "squirm and twist" means. Mostly I want to hear his heartening voice. His name is Omer, but everyone calls him Oats. When I imagine him climbing the massive machinery—which I do, often—he seems too small for a job like that, too handsome and wavy-haired. I imagine his path having crossed Dad's every day at the gates:

Hello, Red!

Hello, Oats!

There's a contract negotiation coming right up, Mr. Vaillancourt explains; a tough one. Management wants change and the papermakers don't. The United Pulp and Paperworkers union has been signing up members, lobbying to replace the existing union.

"Is that what you wanted to know?" he says, standing by the sink in his coveralls, unpacking his lunch pail. I have followed him inside.

"I guess so."

He looks at me. French, soft-spoken, and young, Mr. Vaillancourt isn't much like Dad, but he goes to work on the morning shift like Dad, wears hard-used boots exactly like Dad's. Are my eyes filling? I don't know what I'm after, but he does. "Your father was still one of us," he says.

My father: promoted to foreman but a union man to the bone. A light blinks on inside me.

Mr. Vaillancourt pats my head. "It's good that you're paying attention."

I nod, yes, yes, I'm paying attention! The Vaillancourts, like everybody else, have a *Times* lying out where anyone can pick it up. Sometimes I read it over here. On this day there is likely a front-page photo of the Oxford's president, Bill Chisholm—grandson of the first Hugh Chisholm, son of the second Hugh Chisholm, the third Chisholm to make his way in paper. He's handing out a scholarship, or planting a tree, or cutting a ribbon for the new steam plant or power station or grinding room, always in that good dark suit. A Yale man in heavy, bookish eyeglasses, Bill is in his seventh year at the helm, following the four-decade tenure of his father, the great Hugh II, whose legacy still burns high in the breasts of Mexico's fathers. It was Hugh II who'd run the mill when Dad first saw it; Hugh II who'd rightly predicted that the road to riches would be paved with machine-coated paper. Out with the old machines, in with the new, two million bucks here, four million bucks there, big fat plans undimmed by fire or flood or war or Great Depression. While the rest of America had stood in bread lines, Hugh II's papermakers kept their mill running three and four days a week, heeding their president's advice to place their faith in paper.

Smiling out from another front-page picture in the *Times*, shovel in hand, Hugh II's son Bill has no idea—how could he?—that he's presiding over the beginning of the paper industry's long decline, that the current labor tensions presage a change in the Oxford's fundamental character, one as life-altering as a death in the family.

"You keep it up," Mr. Vaillancourt says to me, which is what adults say to overachieving children.

From outside comes the slamming of car doors, Denise's aunties arriving for their summer visit. They move like starlings in flight, arrowing this way, then that way, in unison, trilling and hooting and cackling and hugging everybody more than once and pattering up and down the stairs to fetch overnight bags and presents and hats, bracelets jangling. I huddle like a stunned dormouse as they circle me, skirts aswirl, Mrs. Vaillancourt introducing me as "Denise's little friend." They are so *enchantée* to meet me. How do you do!

I don't say, *Fine, thank you.* In fact, I say nothing at all. I'm struck dumb, as I often am. Despite my lists of words, my perfect marks in spelling, my desperately thumbed dictionary, I have no vocabulary with which to respond to the kindness that pours in from every quarter. This muteness, and its accompanying well of yearning, fills me with dread. Imagine: a childhood burdened by too much kindness.

The aunties clank their coffee cups and laugh like birds and tell the same stories twice and laugh harder the second time and water up over their own deceased father and sing funny songs in French. They've brought kids with them—Denise's cousins—too many, all ages. I stand at the periphery, memorizing names, but there are too many names, too many people.

At the end of this cacophonous afternoon, I linger outside in the quiet before heading home. Denise is back inside, being quizzed on French words or wheedled into a public performance of *"Je Te Trouve Toujours Jolie"* with her siblings and cousins or asked to report on her hopes for fifth grade. I'm in the yard, picking up my sleuthing notebook, looking over at the empty schoolyard with my own hopes for fifth grade, praying that Sister Bernadette has heard about Dad and therefore will refrain from the obligatory first-day Who Is Your Mother Who Is Your Father get-acquainted routine.

All of a sudden, another little flock from the house, not aunties or cousins, just Denise and Mr. Vaillancourt and Denise's baby sister, Jane. He's going to drive us to the Frosty for an ice cream—before supper, which is unheard-of. Maybe he needs a break from the aunties, who tell chancy jokes in French just to see him blush.

So he drives us to the Frosty. We stand in line. He takes out his wallet and says, "Three vanillas for my girls."

Is this what I've been waiting for? I don't know, then I do.

We get back into Mr. Vaillancourt's Plymouth; he waves out the window to this one and that one. Everybody likes Omer. Sometimes he takes his wife dancing. They play cards with people. They put the words *social* and *life* together in a way I've never heard. It means their friends.

Everyone can see me in Mr. Vaillancourt's Plymouth, eating my ice cream in rude, gulpy, hoggish bites. *Lookit me, everybody!* I say to myself. *Lookit me! Lookit lookit, there's a father at the wheel!* When I get back to their house, I hide in the bathroom, patting my eyes with my fists, as if my eyelashes have caught fire. Outside the door the aunties' laughter sounds like expensive glass breaking. Then I press my eyes so hard the sockets will still ache that night, when I'm lying in bed next to Cathy, wishing she had a best friend with a father like Mr. Vaillancourt. But she doesn't, and neither does Betty, and it's beginning to dawn on me that God might not love all His children the same.

Three vanillas for my girls.

When the union vote happens a few days hence, I record the vote in my blue diary: *UPP wins in a runoff. Labor negotiations can now begin.* These developments barely register in my household, but I have to pay attention now. Because I'm one of Mr. Vaillancourt's girls.

8

Offer It Up

SUMMER PERSEVERES, AS stiff and slow-moving as my mystery book, the adults making what I now see as heroic attempts to soldier on.

Mum's waking hours can't be relied on—"lying down," she calls her sleeping: *I guess I'll lie down for half an hour*—but she manages to fix her hair and make our beds and cook the meals and feed the animals and dress like her lost self. Anne takes us regularly to Dick's Pizza or the Chicken Coop, a restaurant owned by the Kerseys, a fruitful, ruddy family. *Good eatin', that's our greetin'!* We order the "open-faced turkey sandwich," which sounds like something Jackie Kennedy might go for but in fact features soft white bread and a creamy gollup of gravy. We take turns slipping a quarter down the gullet of the booth-side jukebox, which has metal pages you turn by hand. Same song every time: *We'll sing in the sunshine . . . we'll laugh every day. . . .* Hearing us sing along must break our sister's heart. The other fave is "Big Girls Don't Cry."

Anne's a Paul Anka girl who grew up going to "hops," so after we get home one afternoon she teaches us the jitterbug, switching on WRUM, our only radio station.

"Who wants—?"

"Me first me first I called it!" Cathy jaunts to her feet and catches on in seconds. *Kinda showoffy on those underarm turns,* I think. But still. You have to admit: good dancer.

"Now me!" I say.

Anne trades partners while Cathy tries to teach Betty the handhold.

"LIKE THIS?"

"Palms up," Cathy instructs her Pupil. "You're the boy."

"I'M NOT THE BOY."

"Just pretend."

"I'M NOT THE BOY."

Meanwhile, I dance with Anne, her body swaying back and forth—draw back, lean forward, draw back, lean forward—her hands tight in mine. This is how it will be, always, with our sister—close or far, connected always. Gone for weeks in summer to grad school: connected. On a solo trip to Copenhagen or Paris or Stratford-on-Avon: connected. Here or not here: connected. I get the hang of the jitterbug, just as Cathy did, right off, the way I'll get the hang of good posture, and thank-you notes, and subject-verb agreement. Anne can teach anybody anything and make them love what they learn.

Another song comes on: Elvis.

"NOW ME."

"Elizabeth Wood," I announce, "step up to the front, please."

"This isn't School, sweetie," Anne says. "This is dancing.

Take my hand, Bet. You're the *girl*. Now, easy, just rock back and forth."

"She's not rocking."

"Can you hear the beat, sweetie?"

"Her feet aren't even moving."

This is how Betty dances: Like a phone pole. A fence picket. A frozen hen. Hopeless. Worse than Dad, who used to dance wrong to make us laugh.

"She's doing fine," Anne assures us as she jitters and bugs around Betty's stillness, her dainty feet toeing the speckled linoleum. "You having fun, Bet?"

"YUH!"

"Well, isn't that the whole point of dancing?" She is twenty-two years old; Dad's death is so big; she is so small. "There you go, now you're getting it."

Suddenly Mum is here. For a moment she just watches us, then her toe begins to tap.

"TRY IT, MUM!"

She moves like a gorgeous, weary swan, keeping time, keeping time, keeping time.

"WOW, MUMMA!"

"'You ain't nuthin' but a hound dog,'" she sings, and we all laugh, laugh, laugh to hear her old voice, a bright bit of her old self that lasts for sixteen bars.

Father Bob, too, steps it up in this summer of stopped time. Before Dad died, our uncle's visits had been unpredictable—a death, a baptism, a broken church window, so many things could ruin his one day off. But now he arrives every Thursday morning without fail. Like an apparition out of a saint's biography, here he is, waving at us with his pale hands. We charge at him as we used to charge at Dad, vying for his arms.

He's taking us somewhere—it's a surprise—but first he has his coffee with Mum, and then he goes into the parlor to read from his breviary, which he does seven times a day no matter what.

"Mum," Cathy says from the window. "Mumma? Jurgis is peeking in the garbage again."

We look down into the driveway and there's our landlord, his back end sticking out of the trash shed he's recently painted a worshipful shade of green. Square and sturdy as a guesthouse, the trash shed has three doors, one for each floor, which swing open on oiled hinges to reveal a single garbage can for each family. Our cellar, a hair-raising, webby lair with a dirt floor, has similar partitions, the better for the Norkuses to inventory who's wasting what. We keep a potato bag down there, and a few sticks of furniture. The Hickeys, too, keep potatoes and a few oddments, some extra onions. But the Norkuses' section burgeons with great secretive bins of wizening root vegetables, enough to cover all three families in case of an unexpected maraud by the Russian army.

"What do they think I'm throwing away, *babies*?" Mum grumbles. Jurgis extracts a bag of stale doughnuts and *tsk*s so loud we can hear him up here.

The stepped-up garbage rules have forced us into an elaborate cloak and dagger, Mum repacking our trash to hide our offenses—a half-eaten sandwich, a ruined blouse, three-quarters of a bag of cat food in a flavor Tom no longer loves. We squash milk cartons into unassuming flats, squeeze drops of juice from orange peels and apple cores before tossing them, crush the packaging of a new doll or a hand cream inside empty bread bags. But the Norkuses cannot be outwitted. Earlier in the week, like trained hounds, they had sniffed out a housedress from beneath the beef-kidney wrappings and presented it to Mum with an *ash-ash*, *ticka-ticka*, *push-push* of rue. "Missus no throw good dress," Mrs. Norkus said of the piebald thing Cathy had bought for a nickel at the church rummage sale.

"You have to feel sorry for people with that much time on their hands," Mum says, turning away. She puts Father Bob's coffee cup in the sink, then she begins a quick assembly of bologna sandwiches.

Aha. Beach food.

"Yaaay!"

That's the surprise. Father Bob comes back after reading his breviary and confirms it: He's taking us to Reid State Park, all the way to the ocean, which he calls "the surf." Anne has packed our bathing suits into a paper bag.

"Have fun," Mum says. "Behave yourselves." As soon as we leave she'll go to bed.

Once on the road, Father Bob stashes his starchy Roman collar in the glove box but otherwise remains in full regalia: rabat and jacket, black fedora tipped rakishly forward. At the park he'll change into his plaid swim trunks and walk us to the beach in his shiny black shoes.

On Route 2 he starts a round of Elephant in the Road, a car game we've long outgrown.

"Look, girls, an elephant in the road!"

"WHERE?"

"Where?"

"Where?"

"Whoopsy, you just missed it."

"DARN!"

"Darn!"

"Darn!"

"I'm just doing it for Betty," I whisper to Cathy.

"Me, too. This is way too baby."

But really we're doing it for him. He wishes we could stay little.

"Holy smoke, a kangaroo!"

"WHERE?"

"Where?"

"Where?"

Even Betty knows we've got zero chance of spotting a kangaroo on Route 2, but we all look anyway. Because you never know. If an elephant or kangaroo revealed itself to somebody driving along in a car, then that Somebody would be Father Bob and that Car would be this one.

At the Auburn tollbooth, Cathy shouts, "Collar!"

Father Bob snaps open the glove box, grabs the white collar, and reaffixes it with one hand.

"Go right ahead, Father," says the nodding toll man. "No charge."

We sit up like ladies, pretending to be Caroline Kennedy, the privileged daughter of our Catholic president, slipping on through for free. Does it smooth the edges of our uncle's anguish to know his girls are still capable of being thrilled, that they love the fact of the car barely pausing?

Over the years he's taken us "up the pond," "down the pond," to the ocean, to the hills, over the New Hampshire border to Storyland and Santa's Village. For as long as we can remember he's come home to us from his parish in Westbrook or New Gloucester or Hampden or Dover-Foxcroft, a new assignment every couple of years, a perpetual lifting up and setting down of roots and friendships, facing the vagaries of a new parish council, a new congregation, a new housekeeper to train with diplomatic precision, a new home in which to settle his big fat fussy cats. With each impending change we've lain in our beds praying, *Oh please pick Mexico, oh pleasepleaseplease pick Mexico*. But the bishop never picks Mexico. The diocese puts plenty of distance between their men and the appealing distractions of family, a distance that means nothing to Father Bob, who has driven and driven from all these places, only to pick us up, pack us up, and drive some more.

At Reid State Park he lugs his Coleman cooler to a heat-splintered picnic table, then herds us into a frigid, marrow-numbing surf where despite his bad back he surrenders to our demand to be heaved into the lacy waters over and over, his hands threaded beneath our feet, *heave ho! heave ho!* as we bullet skyward and then plunge back down, breathless and alive.

He rubs our hair dry with the beach towel, then opens the cooler and passes out bologna sandwiches and bottles of Moxie. "Boys oh boys, aren't these good," he says. His eyes are watering and pinkish. "Aren't these good, girls?"

"Yes, Fath!"

"Are you having fun?"

"Yes, Fath!"

"Are you sure?"

"Yes, Fath!"

Now the cookies, as many as we want. His blurred emotions are too much for him, but he's trying so hard. Twenty-four years older, Dad had been the father Father Bob always wanted. But we are the children Father Bob always wanted, and he must give to us the solace he himself requires. He makes us wait twenty minutes, then *Back we go, girls, heave ho! heave ho!*, managing somehow to laugh and make us laugh in turn, until he says, *Well, girls, I guess it's time to shove off,* and now we're on the long ride back, the three of us sun-achy and good-tired, our skin salt-tight and humming, our uncle joking at the wheel—*Holy smoke, a wolf and a zebra!*—our day with him almost over and a whole week to wait for the next one. We love our uncle, to whom we are always saying goodbye. Back through the tollbooth— "*collar!*"— back to Mexico, where he drops us off before suppertime and takes another coffee before resuming the long drive back to his rectory and his parish and his cats and his table set for one, always going, going, going, either fleeing from or moving toward, who can tell. I am not yet old enough to understand that despair is the disease and motion is the cure.

"Bye, Fath! Bye, Fath!" we shout from the yard, and as his car rounds the corner and disappears, we bolt into the neighborhood to show off our sunburns before it's time to come back in to eat.

I'm the first one back, announcing to Mum, "Jurgis is peeking in the trash again."

"Offer it up." She opens the cupboard. "How does macaroni and tomato soup sound?"

"Yaaay!" Our favorite meal to top off a wonderful day.

Now Cathy comes in, her cheeks reddened, her T-shirt a mess; she's been making mud houses at the Fergolas'. Mum moves through the kitchen in her new way, slowly, as if the floor itself might give way. She's stranded, afraid, unschooled in the work of being a widow. Whom do you look to? How is this done? She doesn't know, which is why, on this day of heavy garbage inspection, an insult she has already "offered up," she goes a little mad when Betty comes in last, telling us all she's made a friend, a little girl named Susie, but Mrs. Norkus said NO BRING FRIEND.

"She said *what*?" Mum's teeth grit hard. "She said *what*?" Reaching over me, she snaps the window all the way up, a violent ripping sound. Mum looks down; the little friend has already run home.

What is Mum doing now? Offering it up? Sending her

helpless wrath to God? Her delicate jaw vibrates; she jams her fists into her apron pockets and lets them quiver there.

We stare at her. "Mum? Mumma?"

But she's someplace else, utterly lost to us. She picks up the kitchen phone—the only phone—a yellow wall phone that in this charged moment looks radioactive. And unnecessary. At this volume Mrs. Norkus can hear Mum just dandy, phone or no phone, through two floors and two ceilings.

"What's the matter with you!" Mum shouts. "What's the matter with you!"

Through the receiver comes a *push-push* of anger, a torrent of pulped syllables.

Ticka-ticka-too-much-stairs-push-push-you-make-listen!

"No, *you* listen!" Mum cries. "*I'm* telling *you!*"

We can't believe what we're hearing, our soft-spoken mother in a bellow of rage. A full-out explosion now, each woman out-shouting the other, a confusing mash-up of words we know and words we don't.

"Don't you tell me!"

Ticka-ticka-no-bring-push-push-too-much-make-noise!

"My children need friends!" Mum shouts back. "Children need friends!"

Our mouths drop open, one-two-three, as our only mother, in a complete loss of her three-months-long composure, shrieks at our landlady, who must surely believe the Russians have come at last. "And another thing! The garbage is none of your business! It's *my* business! You understand? *My* business!"

Ash-ash—

Bang! goes the receiver as Mum smashes it back into its cradle.

We stare at our mother, our own selves vibrating with fear

and shock and a stitch of pride. Then Mum yanks a chair from the table and sits. *Ohhh*, she sings. *Ohhh*.

Instinctively, we glance around for Anne, but Anne's at the Chicken Coop with Norma. We crowd my mother, petting her hair, eyeing each other.

"Sweet Mother of Mary," Mum says. She covers her face. "Evicted now for sure." She drops her hands and stares at the phone.

We wait, holding our breath.

The phone does not ring. Enraged footsteps do not sound on the stairs.

For days we wait.

Nothing happens.

"I guess we'll make out all right," Mum says, finally.

Because the Wood family, in one form or another, has inhabited the third floor of the Norkus block since the day Dad carried his scrawny bride up too much stairs.

Because the Norkuses know, better than anyone, that once you lose the first essential thing, all things become essential.

Because the Norkuses, who guard their driveway and their trash cans and their flower pots and their stair treads, have apparently included their widowed tenant and her *too much make noise* girls among their guarded things held close.

Come August, as summer begins to unwind, the Norkus rules go a little squishy, still in place but spottily enforced. Denise dodges the rules enough times to try the entire repertoire of Mum's cakes and pies, which Mum offers in fulsome chunks to my friend, my consolation, my good eater. For my part, I take as many meals on Brown Street as I can politely manage, and when the union accepts a one-year, record-high contract, I hear the news at the Vaillancourts' supper table, where the Oxford intrudes as a nearly human presence, almost family.

On my tenth birthday, a week later, I smuggle not only Denise but also my friend Margie upstairs for cake and ice cream. Mum bakes a two-layer cake and gets all dressed up, pearls and everything; Cathy blows out half my candles and I don't even care. Presents galore this year, two paint-by-numbers and a Tammy doll with platinum hair, but nothing compares to my gift from Anne, a Bible with a red leather cover, its pages trimmed in gold. Not one of those little-kid Bibles; a real one. A beautiful book that's all mine. "These are the oldest stories in the world," she tells me. I hold the book and feel its solemn weight.

Leafing through the silky pages, I recognize some of the stories, in versions different from the cleaned-up tales I've heard from the nuns. Violence and vengeance hither and yon, but also charity and hope. They're all in here, all the stories ever told.

It is then that I finally give up on my own book, not because it's been written before—over twenty times, by Carolyn Keene—or because the Bible stories are so much better. Instead, I give up out of sheer exhaustion: I can't figure out why my Missing Man disappeared. I'd planned multiple scenarios for his return (found by Nancy on ocean liner; found by Nancy in haunted hotel; found by Nancy on abandoned cattle ranch), but why did he vanish in the first place? My imagination had failed me there. In the Bible people suffered floods and famine and myriad plague-ridden consequences for inciting the wrath of God. Even when God was *nice* it was no picnic: Noah got to skirt the flood, but he also had to pick only two giraffes out of thousands of giraffes, two chickens out of millions of chickens, two ants out of billions of ants. How did he shore up under that burden? "You," he had to say. "And you. Sorry, that's it, no more squirrels."

Like Noah, my missing man had done nothing wrong. He'd been a good man, with a pleasant wife and a noble collie and a job as an insurance salesman. He had not been lost in a flood or plagued by locusts or swallowed by a whale. He was, simply, gone.

I'd written chapter upon chapter of my book on Oxford paper, ripping sheets in half and starting over, adding copious, not-secret illustrations that I'd sometimes granted Cathy the right to color, though our Crayola set had no crayon called "titian." (Cathy, infuriatingly, used orange.) Betty had no role in the making of my book because the tale took place in a season without snowmen, an oversight I hadn't noticed until it was too late.

In the end, it doesn't matter. I show my book to no one. Mysteries are stupid, I conclude. You have to pretend to believe impossible things. How can a teenage girl get tied up by Suspicious Characters in each new case and undo the knots every time? Besides, isn't the real Nancy too young to drive? Couldn't she miss her mother, at least once? After all my fervid imitations, I'm weary of Nancy's sorrow-proof life, her repeating arc of victory set into type and published a million times over, a fraud of perfection that God Himself hasn't the least whiffling power to change.

So, in this waning summer, I switch to writing "plays" patterned after the French *dictées* I encountered in Sister Ernestine's classroom. The speakers in my dramas are usually sisters, their dialogue shot through with pearly, snootyboots expressions lifted from the Marches and the Cuthberts and the Drews.

Then comes a day when I find only a few sheets left in the packet, so I go to the cupboard for more. When I lift the latch, the door swings open to an unspeakable sight.

No paper.

I gape into the empty larder, gut rising to my throat.

Out of paper.

Out. Of. Paper.

Of *paper*.

The first stage of grief is denial, and I suppose I imagined that last ream as an endless one. We'd wanted for nothing since Dad died—we still had homemade pies and dough-nuts and our animals and all the other people we loved. So we blundered forth in our heedless habit of extravagance, the usual pileup of Cathy's princesses and horses, Betty's snowmen, my artless prose.

I shut the cupboard door, rushing a frantic, begging prayer to St. Anthony, then open it again.

Still bare.

I dare not tell Mum, so I tell Cathy. How, oh how, did we let Dad's paper disappear? How, oh how, will we now acquire more? We do not understand that paper is some-thing you can buy. Despite our ahead-of-grade reading, we've been sheltered by the times, our Catholic education, our priest uncle, our embracing big sister, our mother and father. We do not know the facts of life; we still believe in Santa Claus; we leave room on the couch for the Guardian Angel and regret having no remaining baby teeth to offer the Tooth Fairy. Dad's paper is gone and we know of no way to get it back.

How I ache for all those wasted pages; grief is not too strong a word for that ache. I suppose that up until this mo-ment I believed, somewhere deep, that he could still come back. All those boring identical snowmen, all those stupid princesses with their big fat dresses, all my own vapid pages tossed out because of false starts and misspelled words and dimwitted clues and unlovely illustrations. We have six sheets left and I take them all, hoarding them, writing smaller and smaller, using both sides. With the last, luscious sheet, I revert to my earliest form of meditation, writing a single word over and over, absorbing the form, the feel, the meaning, the rhythm, the sheer sensual jolt of pen on paper.

Deceased. Deceased. Deceased. Four months to the day, and it's still true.

9

The Mystery of the Missing Man

AT THE END of that first Dadless summer, during the last bright sticky days of August, the Vaillancourts head "up the pond" for a week. I have an open invitation to come for a swim, but with no driver in our household I've got no way to get there. Instead of leaving me to fret by myself, Cathy and Betty forgive me my miserly, summer-long refusal to share my secret codes, my secret stakeouts, my secret book, my secret family; *Come with us,* my darling sisters say.

They've spent much of their summer at the Gagnons', another house stuffed with girls whom we've played with since we were old enough to leave the yard. Mrs. Gagnon, the neighborhood beauty; Mr. Gagnon, a woodsman who comes and goes in his wool cap, his face craggy with sun and wind. Mr. Gagnon speaks no English that I know of and seems too big for his house, unlike Dad, who had fit us exactly.

Not everyone in Mexico works at the mill, even though it often seems that way. If you don't make paper, then you're a woodsman like Mr. Gagnon, or a butcher like Mr. Lavorgna, or a nurse or a lawyer or a secretary or a roofer or a schoolteacher or a repairman or a realtor or a bookkeeper or a *Times* reporter or a waitress or a grocery clerk or an insurance agent or a nun.

Either that, or your game is shoes.

We have one small factory in town—we call it the "shoe shop." Other shops flourish within driving distance in all directions, filled with lifers who've punched in every day for years, decades. Stitchers and antiquers and machine tenders and leather cutters, who cut first from the back and hind of the hide, leaving the shanks for the trimmy parts like tassels and tongues. Mothers and fathers inspect vast mats of tanned hide for nicks and wrinkles, the ghostly print of a cattle brand, a stray hair follicle, a half-erased scar. Flawless hides make flawless leather and flawless leather makes flawless shoes. Like Maine-made paper, a Maine-made shoe results from the laying on of hands. Many, many hands. Despite the noise and danger and varnished air, shoemakers, like papermakers, deeply admire the polished fruit of their labors.

Shoemakers like Mrs. Gagnon, on the other hand, bring their work home. Once a week she drives to Rumford to the pickup/drop-off on Waldo Street, where she and the other pieceworkers, mostly women, gather up cumbersome cartons stuffed with shoe parts—uppers and lowers, shapeless leather flaps. Mrs. Gagnon has long arms roped with muscle, strong narrow hands veined from overuse. During her weeklong training session she'd learned the rules, which go like this: Limit, forty paid hours a week. Limit, twenty cases of shoes, thirty-six shoes per case. That's a wage of $2.45 per case. Even for a nimble, experienced stitcher, a case requires at least two hours, with help. And so Mrs. Gagnon, like most pieceworkers, had come directly home to train her kids in turn.

The Gagnon girls—Jocelyne and Liliane, both blondish and a little older; and Francine, my age, with her mother's smoky dark eyes—are nearly as adept as their mother at sewing shoes. After weeks in the company of the Vaillancourts, I follow my obliging sisters back to the Gagnon sewing circle—lively and generous and lighted with the singular thrill of a grown-up job well done. Our task is to stitch the toe end of a loafer, which is a lot harder than it sounds.

How to sew a shoe: Take an upper flap from one soaking bucket, a lower flap from the other. Water relaxes the leather. Select your implements, which are so comely and alluring you'll remember them all your life: a hard white bar of wax; a weighty needle with a generous eye; a length of rawhide drawn from a coiled skein; a padded leather glove, clumsy and fingerless. No matter how small your hand, there's a glove in your size. Prep the rawhide for threading by drawing it in whippy little strokes across the wax. The fuzzy hide will slick right up. Now, take your upper flap, match its machine-punched holes to the ones in the lower flap, and work the needle through this first set of holes. Mrs. Gagnon—whom you adore—will start you off, and then it's up to you.

Pinch the leather as you'd pinch a piecrust, then *zzzip* the rawhide through the holes—the glove will protect your palm from rope burn—and yank tightly enough to force the shape to hold. Do this over and over, thirty-two times, thread-pinch-*zzzip*, thread-pinch-*zzzip*, making even, sprightly stitches, feeling a little kick as this flat, lifeless thing finds its form, an arc that starts at the pinky toe and ends on the opposite side, where a satisfied customer's bunion will not hurt at all in a shoe this watchfully made.

Mrs. Gagnon will check your work by jutting her own needle into your stitches to test their fastness. She'll smile with her entire fine-boned face, tell you *Bon*, *merci*, then complete the tie-off with a whip-quick flourish that fills you with awe.

Your shoe is good. Its toe end looks wearable, its back end still a hapless flap that's not your concern. Toss it into the "done" box, which heaps up rewardingly until you've passed an entire afternoon without noticing where it went.

We have no way of knowing that we're learning a craft just in time to see it vanish. The *zhhr zhhr zhhr* of sewing machines in Taiwan and South Korea is too far away to hear as we take another set of shoe parts from the box. The leather feels alive in our hands: resilient and willing, just like us.

The Gagnon girls, deft enough to add to the "done" box without their mother's inspection, do not cast aspersions on Cathy and me, flub-fingered amateurs by contrast. A done shoe is a done shoe, no matter how long it takes, each identical stitch a little sunbeam of triumph. Those toe ends are faultless and we know it. A handsome arc of identically made stitches, shiny with human sweat. Every Sunday we're reminded that we embarked on a journey at the moment of our baptism, a journey that follows a pitted, potholed, booby-trapped road to heaven. What we wear on our feet, I figure, is no trifling matter.

We take dancing breaks to the stack of 45s on the Gagnons' record player. Mrs. Gagnon has little else to offer by way of reward. We boogie down to "Oh, Sweet Pea," or sit in doleful silence for the whole of Frankie Valli's "Rag Doll," about a beautiful poor girl from the wrong side of the tracks. Betty joins us sometimes; she loves the Gagnons' baby sister, Jacqueline. They fill coloring books or push Jaci's doll carriage up and down the driveway. Neither of them is allowed to sew, but they dance with us (Betty like a phone pole, Jaci like a cricket) and join in the end-of-sewing-time treat: white bread, larded and salted on both sides, then fried in Mrs. Gagnon's big black pan. She calls this "toast."

At week's end Mrs. Gagnon hangs the finished shoes on round metal hooks, making circular bundles like giant key chains. One by one she hefts them over her knotted shoulder, loads her car, and drives to Rumford to pick up another batch.

Mum doesn't wholly approve of our sewing shoes now. What if the neighbors think we're actually employed, her little urchins earning bread money? But Mum understands the curative power of work, remembers how Dad admired our tiny calluses. And this besides: She admires Mrs. Gagnon's beauty and resolve; and, she likes shoes. She wears pretty ones even in the house, shoes with shiny toes or butterfly bows or maybe a kitten heel. They come in different colors, a little shock in the colorless land of grief, every tick of her heel a reminder that she still exists.

The *Times* continues to provide a trove of information, much of which I don't understand. "What does 'feet of clay' mean?" I ask Father Bob, here for his weekly visit. I've been muddling through an article about the mighty Oxford's unraveling rapport with its rank and file.

Father Bob is drinking Mum's coffee and teaching Cathy the fine points of card shuffling while I study the paper, waiting my turn. Feet are feet, Father Bob explains, and clay is clay, but when you put them together it means finding out that people you think are perfect in every way turn out to have a Tragic Flaw. I can think of only one "person" who's perfect in *every* way, since even Father Bob barks at us on occasion. "Jesus, you mean?"

"Jesus doesn't have feet," Cathy says. "He's invisible."

Father Bob laughs his ho-ho-ho laugh, which floats over us like a cloud filled with sunlight, reinforcing my elevated impression of our place in God's esteem. As an ordained priest in the Roman Catholic Church, Father was born to be God's stand-in on earth, and if he thought we three were cuter than cute . . . ? I modestly left it to others to draw the obvious conclusion.

"Then who? Mum?"

He chuckles. "No."

She's standing right here, and we all agree that if any mortal could be deemed perfect in every way, it would be Mum. And Anne. And Father Bob, of course. Possibly the cat.

"Sister Edgar?"

"No."

"SISTER EGGER?" Betty offers.

"Betty, I just said that."

"MRS. NORKUS AND JURGIS?"

Father is laughing it up now, his forehead reddening.

Mum gives her brother a look. "Those people came to America with rags on their feet."

Again with the feet. "Who then?" I ask. "Who has feet of clay?"

But Father can't, or won't, think of anybody, and so my quest for the Tragically Flawed roaming among us goes unrequited until the last Thursday in August, the mill pumping out chewable air that hangs low over our valley. Mrs. Gagnon has a batch of shoes to finish before day's end, but we forsake our pastime to wait at home for Father Bob. Who is late.

"There's his car!" Cathy announces.

"Yaaay!"

From our back door she's glimpsed it moving down Mexico Avenue. Odd. Not his usual route. We wait. And wait. He hasn't missed one single Thursday since Dad died. We get our bathing suits out, a blow-up ring for Betty. And wait some more.

"It must have been somebody else's car," Mum tells her.

"Nuh-uh. It was his. Blue and white."

"There are lots of blue-and-white cars."

Actually, there aren't. Father Bob always has a good-looking car in an eye-catching color. Cathy is stubborn and smart and bossy and you can't put a thing over on her. "Let's go get him," she whispers. There's only one other place he could be.

"We shall pursue his trail," I say, or something like it.

"You can't come if you're gonna act like Nancy."

"I'm not acting like Nancy."

"Are too. Nobody says 'shall.'"

Chastened, I agree not to say "shall." Here's an actual mystery, at last—Father Bob's never late—but it's not the thrill I might have been hoping for. No thrill at all. I feebly suggest a flashlight, but Cathy says that's acting like Nancy and anyway it's one o'clock in the afternoon. So we set off for our aunt and grandfather's house, averting our eyes when we pass the Venskus block where Dad's brand-new Chrysler waits in its bay, untouched since April. We step it up and keep going, and in two minutes we're planted on Cumpy and Aunt Rose's sloping porch, staring in disbelief at the door.

"It's locked," Cathy says.

So extraordinary is this news that it leaves me speechless. I sprint around the side of the house and come back with more news: "His car is here."

The front door has a long oval window covered from the inside with a crummy lace curtain. We try to see through the holes. Aunt Rose and Cumpy aren't home. But Father Bob's in there. We know he is.

"Knock on the door."

"*You* knock."

"No, you."

Like cats used to indulgent owners, we do not know what to make of a locked door in the middle of the afternoon. Finally Cathy knocks. Nothing. Then we both start knocking—polite, small-fisted inquiries.

Finally, the curtain parts and there's Father Bob's face. Or, his face plus a Tragic Flaw, his eyes so wrong, so not his, so cloudy and unfocused they seem to be floating in his head. Like eggs. Like big fat eggs. At the same time he looks stricken, blinking at us through the window. He drops the curtain and we see him again through the scrim of lace.

We stand there, our hearts skittering, trying to make sense of our world gone all awhack. Finally he opens the door. "Girls!" he says, his customary gladsome greeting. But the word slushes out as if uttered under water, a sodden mouthful of *l*'s. I think: *This can't be him. Maybe this isn't him.*

It's him, all right. He moves backwards, on tippy toes, his clay feet weaving to and fro.

"Fath, what's wrong?"

"Nothing, girllls!" he gurgles. He's wearing his priest pants with a wrinkled white undershirt.

"Why didn't you come over?"

"Cathy saw your car. We waited and waited."

"Fath, what's the matter?"

"Nothing, girllls. Nothing, nothing, nothing."

Cathy's mouth opens, rubbery and soft. "Father Bob! Father Bob! Are you sick? Monnie, I think he's sick!"

Father, I think, *you're going to have to pull yourself together.* But I can't say it aloud. "Let's go, Cath, let's tell Mum."

"No-oh-oh," he says, another watery mouthful. He totters into my aunt's cluttered parlor, a dreadful little two-step, like a cartoon character weaving out of a saloon—exactly like that, a character with eggs for eyes and a stream of bubbles emanating from his head. He tries to put his features in the proper order, then reels backwards with the effort.

"He's drunk!" I gasp, finally believing my eyes. "Cathy, he's drunk!" We have never once beheld a drunk person but apparently we're looking at one now. I feel like a stepped-on flower.

"He's not *drunk,*" snaps my know-it-all sister. "He's *dancing!*"

I leave her crying there and sneak down the short hall that leads to the kitchen. Cumpy's cat, a sumptuous orange coon cat named Roddy, sits on the counter, batting at a long, clear, empty bottle. It spins in a slow, mesmerizing circle, right in place. I've never seen a bottle like this except on TV, but I know it's liquor, and I know that liquor makes cartoon characters dance exactly the way Father Bob is dancing. I kiss Roddy on the face, listen to his guttural purring—we call it "singing"—and close my eyes. *Whiskey,* I think: the only liquor I've heard of. Whiskey! Father Bob, Perfect in Every Way, drank a bottle of whiskey.

I hug the singing cat. Think! Think! Do you die from drinking a bottle of this?

I fly into the parlor and yell at my sister, who is still crying, begging Father to tell her what's wrong with him. So I tell her again.

"I saw a bottle! He drank a whole bottle!"

"No-oh-oh," says Father, crying now. Our adored uncle, our priest-in-the-family, God's stand-in, once again bawling like a baby.

"I saw it, Cath! I think it's whiskey!"

No he didn't yes he did no he didn't.

Then she looks at him again. Yes he did.

I tug at her shirt. "Come on, Cath, we have to tell Mum."

She doesn't want to go. Father Bob is sacked into a chair like a deflated beach ball, the parlor a suffocating cave filled with knickknacks and cat hair, the blinds drawn tight. "What if he's sick? What if he's sick? What if he—?"

I drag her out to the porch, where we shut the ugly door behind us and gallop home, breathless and wailing, thundering up the stairs past the silent Norkuses. How will we tell Mum? What if she cries? What if she says something terrible and life-turning like *He's dead, isn't he?*

"Mum!" Cathy cries. "Mumma!"

We tell our tale but Mum doesn't even look surprised. Her slow, cheerless, head-shaking smile baffles us. On this day our loved ones' faces are doing strange, strange things. "He's sad, that's all," she says. "He's very sad." Her arms come around us. "Don't worry, he'll make out all right."

But we won't be so easily consoled, and as that ruined day crawls to a close, Cathy and I whisper in our bed about what we've seen, careful to stay under the covers so Betty can't hear.

The next morning we open our swollen eyes to find Father Bob, in his blacks and collar, standing at the foot of our bed. He can't speak, his face jellying with emotion, his hair wet-combed and slicked back, his jaw shaved too close, pink-pink and slapped-looking. We sit up, our hearts thundering. What do we do now?

"Can you forgive me?" he stammers.

"Yes, Father!" we cry, and bolt up, hugging him around the neck as he blubbers into our pajama collars.

"I'm sorry," he keeps saying, "I'm sorry I'm sorry." He smells of peppermint and Aqua Velva and sweat.

"That's enough," Mum says, coming in. "They forgive you. You want something to eat?"

We all do. I sit at the table, eating my oatmeal, the bird perched on the rim of my bowl, flicking out the raisins. Nobody says much. I eat slowly, taking surreptitious peeks at my uncle, who looks the same as always, handsome and put together, no resemblance to the dancing man we saw yesterday. Against the rules, I teeter back in my chair, the better to slide a glance at his feet, which are not shod in clay at all but in a black, spit-shined pair of Maine-made wingtips.

Then Mum says, "You want some more?" and he says, "Are you trying to make me fat?" and Betty says, "YOU'RE A BIG FAT EGG," and we all laugh, and the surreal feeling of that locked-door day begins nearly at once to fade.

He will tell me, in time, that this day was his turning point. It is also mine. As I watch him come back to himself, a feeling visits me, an odd warmth that I don't yet recognize as the essence of family love: the power to bestow forgiveness, to turn trespass into redemption, to stitch a lasting shape out of formless sorrows, even in a season already steeped in grief.

He comes back on the following Thursday, same as always, clean-shaven and wet-combed and shoeshined, to take us up the pond or down the pond. And then, just as school resumes in September, he disappears.

10

~

Just Nervous

H<small>E CAN'T MAKE</small> it today, Mum said the first week.
The second week: Last Rites. Can't make it.
The week after that: Bishop visiting. Can't be helped.

And again: Parish council meeting.

And now here we are, in full autumn, and he's missed another Thursday. We haven't seen Father Bob once since school started—fifth grade for me, third for Cathy; and third for Betty because Mum's decided to keep trying.

The days snap open anyway, in that distinctive way of fall days, short and crisp, a sensation of change afoot. But nothing changes. Mum's grief is less visible, perhaps, but her muted shame endures as a tender darkness in these shortening hours, the light vanishing in more ways than one.

In the *Times* I read that the Strand is showing Kirk Douglas in *20,000 Leagues Under the Sea;* that the Mexico Pintos suffered their first loss of the year after the quarterback broke his collarbone; that the sensational Impacts will be playing all weekend in the Rainbow Room at the Legion hall. I read that the governor of Maine addressed the Sons of Italy on Thursday night, calling out the "ruthless Communist effort" as our greatest threat. To Bill Chisholm, who hosted the long-service banquet at the Rumford armory, our greatest threat was "competition." Nine hundred papermakers looked up from their mashed potatoes as the Oxford's third president announced a fifty-million-dollar expansion "to ensure our future."

Can Dad see all this from heaven?

"Sister Bernadette says life goes on," I say to Anne. We're halfway through October, the ever-starched collar of my school uniform already wilting with wear.

"Life does go on, sweetie. It has to." She's at the kitchen table, tabulating grades on her adding machine, a refurbished thirty-pound brute Dad bought only months ago. He'd touched it, paid for it, carried it home for Mum to wrap as a gift to their schoolteacher daughter. I love the sound—especially at night when I'm in bed—a muscular clacketing that means Anne is out there.

"I miss Fath."

"He's busy, that's all," she tells me. "It's hard to be a pastor."

I sidle up to the table. "I want everything to go back how it was." Before Dad, I mean. I blush at the unseemly baby-whine in my voice.

Anne pulls out her chair and gathers me into her lap, which is too small for me now. I've shot up over the summer, suddenly too big for her body. "We have two choices," she says, holding me fast. "We can ask why-why-why, over and over. Why-why-why?" She pauses, letting that useless plea sink in. "Or," she says, "we can just *do*."

I well up. "I don't want to just *do*."

She waits; this is how I always know she's listening. Then: "Monnie," she whispers. "Just doing doesn't hurt as much as why-why-why."

Of course she's guessed what I've privately been asking God for. Sometimes I ask nicely — *O merciful God, O heavenly Father* — and sometimes I don't — *Give him back! I mean it! Right now!* I've also asked God's army of surrogates — the Virgin Mary; Jesus the Son; the angel Gabriel; St. Anthony, who's good at finding things; and my own patron saint, St. Monica, whose claim to sainthood was to pray endlessly for her degenerate son, Augustine, to become a writer and saint remembered through the ages. Twenty years later God finally said to St. Monica: *Oh, all right. Happy now?*

I slip off my sister's knees, infused with a resolve to do better, to be better. I finish October by writing the inaugural issue of the fifth-grade newspaper for several days running, spread out in the parlor with Denise, my co-editor. We gather all the news, write all the articles, draw all the comics, choose the weekly prayer. We use Oxford paper — store-bought by Anne — which doesn't smell the same. As Mum reads all four pages with her brow rumpled in admiring concentration, I begin, possibly for the first time, to perceive accomplishment as a way out of despair. At school I launch into spectacular overreach, reading ahead by chapters not pages, staying for *ménage* not once a week but every day, keeping my school desk a model of godliness, spritzing it daily with a lime-green fluid Sister Bernadette keeps in the cupboard. For a show-and-tell on Africa, Denise and I use up a month's worth of *Times* back issues to make a papier-mâché topographical map, slopping water on Mum's parlor rug and leaving strips of paper stuck to the chairs. The finished map is so huge and unwieldy that as we wrestle it down over the first-floor landing, the Norkuses go mute with befuddlement. The messy projects tend to unfold in my household, and the neat ones—we're teaching ourselves guitar on Silvertones bought at Montgomery Ward—in hers.

This is called "doing." This is called "not asking why-why-why." But it is not—not exactly—life going on.

Coming home after school one Friday near Halloween, I open the door to find the kitchen empty, the radio off, the parakeet muttering under his breath. Is this when I first notice the absence of song? That sound I'd been hearing all summer—was it the sound of Mum not singing?

"Music is prayer," Sister Louise, our choir director, is fond of saying. "God hears you faster." Cathy and I sing in choir, we sing along to the jukebox at the Chicken Coop, but we don't sing here anymore. At home. In this kitchen, which had once been filled all the live-long day with my mother's voice.

We have a family song—the car-trip song, courtesy of Irving Berlin, a song I haven't heard in a long time. Months. Six months to be exact, back in April when Dad drove us to Lewiston for our annual trip to Peck's, a department store with a beguiling elevator and a luscious array of Easter dresses. Dad tapping the wheel as Anne and Mum swapped roles in a syncopated show tune that demanded concentration and immaculate pitch: *I hear music but there's nooo one there! I smell blossoms but the treees are bare!* Dad's speaking voice had depth and gravel and other consolations, but a singer he was not. He liked to step-dance instead, badly, like a rooster wearing galoshes, a jokey tribute to his PEI roots, *steppity-tappity-bang-bang-BANG*, which made Mum laugh, hard and hooty, every single time. In the car that day he just listened, guiding us along a road that followed our filthy, frothing, flowing river.

These memories well up as I stow my schoolbooks and listen harder to the quiet. Sister Louise's dictum—*Music is prayer*—loops like a melody in my head. Cathy and Betty are at the Fourniers', visiting the pigeons in their coop; Anne's still at school; the ambient sounds of our family at home after a school day have been stilled. Is it this stillness that unnerves me, or merely the weather—a dampening that isn't rain, a thickening odor from the mill, portents of a late burst of Indian summer? As I wait in the softening air, I recognize how long I've missed Mum's singing, how I've pined for it, her stretched notes and dolorous crescendos in "Autumn Leaves" and "You'll Have to Go" and "Tammy," all the most-requested from WRUM.

But all is soundless now. I mouse-creep into my bedroom to find her napping on the bottom bunk with an afghan slung over her shoulders. Across from her, on the bed I share with Cathy, Tom is sacked out on a pillow, also asleep.

"Mum?"

She stirs. The cat stirs.

"Mum? You awake?"

She rouses herself, puts on her glasses, looks at me. The cat sits up and purrs.

"Remember that song?" I ask her. "'I Hear Music'?"

She nods. Her hair's all mashed on one side.

I wait. "'I hear music but there's no one there'? That one?"

She tries to smile, murmuring the song's big finish: "'You're not sick, you're just in love.'"

"Uh-huh. That one."

I wait some more. Nothing happens. So I pick up the singing cat and give him to her.

She kisses his hard fuzzy head. "You're a *goosey* cat," she croons. "You're a goosey goosey *gumdrops*." This is how she talks to animals, in baby talk; we all do. But lately, at odd times, like now, she reverts to her regular voice. "Time to start supper, I guess," she says to him, still sitting on the bottom bunk. "What about hamburg? I've got some hamburg in the fridge." Hearing her gives me the shivers, as I half expect Dad to answer through a slit in the sky.

But neither of Mum's dearest male creatures, only one of whom talks back, can answer for Dad. The parakeet can sing four bars of "Sugartime" and open the gate on his cage, but he can't make our landlords open the gate to the garden. The cat can warm Mum's feet at night but can't lug the oil can upstairs or fix a stogged-up toilet.

Even if Father Bob could magically appear on the instant, he wouldn't be able to do these things either, not with his bad, much-operated-on back. He's famously unhandy, and the Norkuses, cowed by his cassock, behave beautifully in his presence, leaving him no opening to rectify their trespasses. We need Father Bob anyway; if he's not the man *in* the house, he's the man *of* the house. And he's gone, stuck at his parish, because the stupid bishop visited; because the stupid parish council met; because a stupid dying parishioner asked to be anointed.

Is he thinking of us, in his tidy, two-story rectory? It has white steps and a mowed lawn, not unlike the houses from *Dick and Jane*. And cats, too—pliable, affectionate, good-smelling beasts he rescued from the road. Like Nancy Drew, Father Bob has a housekeeper, a bony, aproned woman named Thurza Hines who likes children and makes cookies with M&M smiley faces before smiley faces have a name.

Mrs. Hines doesn't live in, an arrangement that allows Father Bob to do some of his own cooking, and so the guest rooms and housekeeper's digs become ours whenever we visit.

Oh, the splendor of those rooms: the tasseled bedspreads, the white nightstands, the floral curtains, a bathroom to ourselves alone. Since toddlerhood we'd made these visits, each glorious one beginning with a Mass in the church next door, a Mass that looked nothing like a real Mass. We were the only congregants and it was not Sunday and we were not in Sunday clothes. No altar boys. No choir. No homily. No concelebrants. Just our magnificent uncle chanting the Offertory in a sonorous talk-singing that sounded as if it came from an ancient, echoing cave. He consecrated the host, whispering in Latin, sipping the wine till it was gone. Stillness overtook us. This was the awe of God.

After Mass we'd rush the sacristy to watch him shed his vestments, smooth out their gilded folds, and hang them in a closet made special. He stashed the chalice and paten. Everything so tidy, so proper. Each hidden place required a tiny gold key: closet, tabernacle, a cedar cupboard that held the altar linens. This was our first brush with elegance; we learned the after-Mass protocol the way children in other places learned to trim a sail or wax their skis.

Afterwards, our fists clamped around dripping ice-cream cones, we'd stroll through a town not ours where we met parishioners who patted our heads and commended our sterling behavior. We were Father Bob's wonderful girls, his honor and joy, and even in our earliest visits — early enough that I remember having to be lifted into the car — I'd perceived in his presence a dozy, distant weight, the baffling burden of being intensely loved.

Those times with Father Bob seem far away as Mum finally gets up to start supper. I follow her into the kitchen, sick with longing. "When's he coming back, Mum?"

She knows who I mean. "Bye and bye," she says, opening the fridge. She picks up a package of hamburg and stares at it. She looks like a spirit to me, a shimmer of herself: pale, with sky-blue veins netting her temples, a faraway sheen in her eyes. At times I believe I can see clear through her; but at least she's here, right here, close enough that I can put my arms around her and squeeze. Father Bob, on the other hand, is just plain gone. I want to go to the rectory and pretend to be Caroline Kennedy in my frilly white twin bed. Even more, I want him to come to us, to visit my new fifth-grade classroom and drink Mum's coffee and finish teaching me pinochle, a complicated card game that requires two decks I love to shuffle. I want him to drive us overtown where we can strut alongside him, up and down Congress Street to window-shop and then into Razzano's for spaghetti and meatballs and Moxie with ice. I want to follow him into and out of stores where they give him free this and free that because he grew up here and went away to college and did not fail to answer his holy calling. I want to follow him like an imprinted gosling with my gosling sisters and believe he's just like Dad.

"Come," Mum says, shutting the fridge door. As awake as she's going to get. "You can help me set the table."

I look hard at her. "How long is bye and bye?"

She runs her hand over my hair. "You girls have to learn how to wait."

It will take a long time for me to know that Father Bob was not like Dad. For him to be anything like Dad—loose with laughter, physically tough, a natural lightheart—had never been possible. Mum and her siblings came from a family unhappy in all the usual ways: too much whiskey, not enough cash. They'd emigrated from the same PEI county that Dad would forsake a generation later, but unlike Dad's migration, theirs seemed hard-won, half-evolved, unfinished. Who knew why some farmers took to papermaking and some didn't? Maybe it mattered how much you'd loved farming in the first place, or how heavily you grieved for your abandoned, unyielding land. Dad talked about PEI all the time, told all those affectionate tales, made his homeland seem like a celebration he'd carried with him rather than a heartache he'd left behind.

Cumpy told no tales from his former life, not even when his brother and sisters came to visit. He and my unremembered grandmother raised their kids in a Rumford block and in time bought a real house in Mexico, a gabled single-family with a yard, every immigrant's dream. But by then it was too late to renew their faith in happiness, for they'd lost something far more precious than their homeland.

Mum was nine years old on that magically bright Sunday in 1923, skipping along Waldo Street in the September sunshine with her sister Sadie and their angelic baby brother, John James, joined by other children from other blocks, some cousins, some not. Shrieking and laughing, they act like kids from any generation, from any culture or faith, playing hopscotch or kickball in their bubbling pastiche of Franco and Irish and Italian expressions, one kid picking up from another. *Tant pis!* hollers one child, *Capiche?* shouts another, *Quit yer crakin'!* teases another, and like crows on a roadside they pluck these baubles and carry them home to their disapproving parents.

The melting pot boils over at times, but not today. Today is all high, cool sunlight and freshening fall air, the kind of dry, blue-sky day when the mill's stench fades a bit and goodwill bursts from unexpected places. A few hours after Sunday Mass, where they've bent their heads in dutiful supplication, the children have abandoned themselves to the day. A teenager across the street, barely out of boyhood himself, comes out to the stoop, feeling generous, perhaps, after the Gospel reading from the morning Mass: *And He took a child, and set him in the midst of them: and when He had taken him in his arms, He said unto them, Whosoever shall receive one of such children in My name, receiveth Me.* The young fellow sits his lanky self down, straightens his Sunday cuffs, and opens a bag of sweets. He calls across to the cute little four-year-old, Mum's beloved brother, my baby uncle: *You want one, kid?*

Of course he wants one! John James, destined to ascend straight to heaven by virtue of his tender age and Catholic baptism, darts into the path of a luckless neighbor's coughing Model T. His sister screams his name and the whole day dies.

Internal hemmorage from automobile accident, reads the misspelled death certificate signed in a bold, shocked hand by the Rumford town clerk. *Duration: 3 hours. Contributing cause: Nervous shock.*

Three hours it took for little John James to die, and so much longer than that—never, I suppose—for his family to express its pain. Their blue-eyed boy had turned four in July, same birthday as his big sister, who'd given him four playful swats on the bottom—*plus one to grow on!* But it was not to be.

So here is Mum, young Margaret, suffering her little-girl grief, an engulfing shock made worse by the silence that will attend it forever after. Never will she hear his sweet Irish name again. Is it any surprise that the next boy born to the family—a "change of life" baby in more ways than one—will become her pet? They call him Bobby, until the moment of his ordination, when everyone, including Mum, his fourteen-years-older sister, will switch to "Father Bob" in less time than it takes for him to transform wine into the blood of Our Lord Jesus Christ.

The death of John James made everyone more of what they already were: mother sterner and needier and more resentful of her living girls; father heavier-drinking and quicker-tempered; and daughter—Mum—more straight-backed and responsible, more weighted down than ever as the oldest child. The packet of fading photos gives it away if you know how to look: always a rundown porch landing and stair rails behind, always a child squinting into strong sunlight and a grim-faced adult skulking in shadow. What must it have been like to grow up in that silence?

People, like trees, want to grow toward the light, and for Mum, Dad was that light. This was true, too, for Father Bob, a lonely, bookish boy who found in Dad the father he'd always wanted. Maybe Mum did, too, in the older man she'd come to call "Dad," a papermaker with merry blue eyes, the opposite of her brooding, dark-drinking father. A baby brother once himself, Dad took to little Bobby, possibly even wooed Mum by befriending the towheaded little fulla.

Later on they must have made a funny pair, Dad an aging papermaker with his yellow teeth and plaid shirts, Father Bob in the rinsed grace of his young priesthood, with his clean fingernails, his fluency in French and Latin, his taste for classical music, his degree from Holy Cross and Grande Séminaire. I haven't a single memory of them together; like my onetime heroine Nancy Drew, however, I can deduce Father Bob's devotion to Dad by recalling the depth of his heartache.

Perhaps Father Bob had always been a crier, but Dad's

death had unlatched another gate; now my uncle puddled up over striped cats, straight-A report cards, salmon sunsets, Irish singers, God's everlasting love. Even so, I believed he was big and strong when in fact he was fragile, far more fragile than I knew in 1963, when he stumbled by default into the yawning void Dad left behind, a grief-broken priest presiding over the funeral, following the casket with the poise of a sailing ship, his billowing vestments filled with the breath of God.

I suppose he prayed for guidance. Prayed for strength. He typed out the Serenity Prayer from Alcoholics Anonymous and taped it into his breviary. Seven times a day he opened the supple leather cover and saw that prayer. *God grant me the serenity to accept the things I cannot change . . .* First he bent, and then he bent some more, and then he broke.

The Catholic tradition of my childhood—which I recall with affection, some awe, and a measure of yearning—did not allow for randomness. Every word and deed, every sorrow and triumph, every birth and death belonged to a Divine Plan. If at times you thought this Plan unreasonable, senseless, or just plain mean, you were asked to trust that even the most extreme sorrow had to be a blessing in disguise. Almost everything essential came to you in disguise. Everything that happened was part of something beyond your human ken, a necessary preparation—for what, remained to be seen. Best case: something better. Worst case: something worse.

Wherever you fit into this plan—giving Communion or receiving Communion; top of the class or mentally retarded; working or on strike; whole and happy or hacked to pieces by grief—you *fit*. That was the Plan's cruel beauty. You wept if you had to, hid your face and gnashed your teeth, but you knew that if you repaired to your bed of pain it was because God wanted you there—only you; only there—to complete the unknowable requirements of something great and vast and ultimately beautiful.

Believe it or not, this was a comfort.

Sometime—not long—after I ask for the "I Hear Music" song, Mum resumes singing at last. Humming, really, with the occasional full-blown song—"Flow Gently, Sweet Afton," her favorite, about a woman in her stream-side grave. The resumption of singing in our house, even a song as troubling as this, feels like a turning tide.

But it's early November now, and still Father Bob hasn't surfaced.

"Where *is* he, Mum?" I'm not a baby fourth-grader anymore. I want answers and I want them now.

Washing dishes in the pocked double sink, Mum pretends not to hear. "'My Mary's asleep by the murmuring stream,'" she sings. I know the difference between when she can't hear because of her bad ears and when she can't hear because she doesn't like the question.

"Ask Anne," Cathy says.

"Where is he, Annie?"

"He'll be back."

"WHERE IS HE?" That's Betty; now they have to tell.

"In the hospital," Mum says finally.

We look at each other, flabbergasted. Why didn't they just say so? This news is no surprise; this news is nothing! Father Bob's been in the hospital plenty of times: lower back, gallbladder, upper back, kidney stones, you name it, scars all over.

"Can we go see him?"

Father Bob always goes to the hospital in Bangor. Aunt

Rose could drive us; she's like her brother that way: single, drives all over, all the time.

"The hospital's in Baltimore," Mum says. "That's in Maryland. Which is another state far away from here."

But that's not the real reason. We just know it. We move in, crowding her body as she scrubs a pan. Her body is our comfort, so pillowy and warm.

"How far?"

"*Far.* Near Our Nation's Capital." This is how she always refers to President Kennedy's city—reverently, in capital letters.

Cathy uses this information to surmise that Father Bob could be visiting President Kennedy, who's Catholic like us and has a retarded sister like us and is handsome in a Father Bob–ish way. Like most of Cathy's conclusions, this one sounds reasonable enough to me. I picture my uncle watering a tray of pansies affixed to the window of his hospital room, which overlooks the White House lawn where Caroline, just a little bit younger than me, rides her pony in ecstatic circles as her parents watch with their pearly smiles.

Betty's the one who thinks to ask: "WHAT HAPPENED TO HIM?"

"Gallbladder," Cathy says. She always gives the answer.

"You only have one gallbladder," I inform her. "They can't take it out twice."

"His back, then."

"THEY TOOK OUT HIS BACK?"

"He's just nervous," Mum says. She dries the flour scoop, glances at Anne, opens the flour bin, drops it in, la-la-la.

We don't like the sound of this. *Nervous* is a PEI word whose meaning slips around. Aunt Rose gets "nervous" sometimes, when she comes over with her face crimped and

162

red and her eyes popping. Cumpy, too, on occasion. Sometimes Father Bob wears his fedora because we tell him it looks so fancy, but other times he wears it to cover the inflamed scales along his widow's peak. That means nervous. Mum puts Vaseline on his head, which never helps.

But maybe the hospital will fix it. And maybe Father Bob will bless the president, and then the president will invite us to the White House and give us a ride on Caroline's pony. These fancies keep my mind alight for days, until Mum announces at supper one night that instead of Thanksgiving at home next week, we're going on a trip.

What? We've never gone on a trip.

We are now. To the hospital in Baltimore.

"Yaaaay!"

We'll pick up Father Bob in Aunt Rose's car, and then drive to Our Nation's Capital—

"Yaaaay!"

—to see the White House in person, and the Capitol, and the Lincoln Memorial, and the Washington Monument.

We can't believe it. We cannot believe it. We make Mum tell us again.

I make a dash to the Vaillancourts' to crow about our family trip. "We're leaving on Tuesday," I tell Denise. "I get to miss school."

Denise's eyes widen. I have something she wants. This switcheroo floods me with a guilty, luscious light.

"We might meet the president and Jackie and Caroline." I don't care about John-John, who is a boy and not worth mentioning.

"You lucky," Denise says. She's officially jealous, but she still loves me; the moment is exquisite, and the pony ride of my daydream suddenly seems possible.

"We're getting new dresses, too," I add, which might not be true.

Before I get around to asking Mum about a new dress, a man named Lee Harvey Oswald sneaks into a book repository in Dallas, Texas, where he crouches at a sixth-floor window and points a gun and shoots the president dead. What happened to my family in April is now happening to the Kennedys; what happened to the Kennedys is now happening to the whole country; and the whole country cannot stop crying.

11

Widows' Instructions

An hour before Oswald pulls the trigger, I'm at choir practice, knuckling under the tutelage of Sister Louise, a lean, starchy woman who Means Business and Means It Now. For a goodly portion of our lunch hour every day, we stand in the choir loft, straight-shouldered and ladylike, singing into the rich echo chamber of the empty church, learning to sight-read and harmonize and *pro-JECT, pro-JECT, pro-JECT!* Sister Louise sounds out all the parts—not a good voice, though her pitch is flawless, her directing eminently followable. We keep our eyes on her long, lolloping fingers.

The hands stop, shutting us up on the instant.

"Who laughed?" Sister Louise swivels her flushing face from the altos to the soprano IIs to the high sopranos and back again, the scorching heat of her gaze liquefying the innocent and guilty alike.

"I said, who laughed?"

I exchange a sidelong glance with Denise, who stands beside me with the soprano IIs, and another with Cathy, over there with the altos. We know from experience that Sister Louise can hold out longer than Methuselah. She can keep us through the end of the school day if she takes a notion; through supper, through the night, through the feast day of St. Blaise, seventy-three days hence. Our skin will rot away, our hair fall out from starvation, we will petrify ourselves into a choir of singing skeletons, our uniforms gone to rags, and still she'll be there: arms crossed, waiting for the malefactor to confess.

And so: "*I* did, Sister." Linda Cote, sixth grade, possessor of enviably long blond hair and, apparently, a sizable death wish.

"Why were you laughing?"

"No reason, Sister."

"People don't laugh for no reason."

"Well, it sounded kind of funny when your voice cracked."

As Carolyn Keene would have it: *They froze in horror!*

"And you thought that was funny?"

"Yes, Sister." No choice here. She has to tell the truth.

"Is that so? Then perhaps you would do us all the great favor of singing these lines yourself."

Cue the organ, Sister Mary of Jesus (kindly; mustachioed; outranked) staring helplessly at the sheet music. A brief intro, slow and funereal. Then Linda sings four bars like a springtime sun, her voice warm and pure and touched by a faint, angelic vibrato. *Tantum ergo Sacramentum, Veneremur chernui. . . .*

Uh-oh.

"Well, students? Was that funny? Linda, did you hear anybody laughing while you sang?"

"No."

"No?"

"No, Sister."

Wherever Sister Louise might have been going with this, she appears to have lost her way. Perhaps she's been blindsided by the eerie joy of a young girl's clarity of tone, or by the revelation that she, Sister Louise, has created a thing of beauty out of a mixed crew of schoolgirls who came to her with zero musical chops and wound up singing like the Cherubim and Seraphim. She teaches school because she has to; she directs the choir because she loves to. Her choir—our choir—is *good*. We've been told, by Sister herself, that we channel the sweetness of heaven.

"All right, then," she says, glaring briefly at Linda, then at Sister Mary of Jesus, pretending she's nailed down her murky point. "Now. Everyone. From the first measure." She lifts her hands, thumbs and index fingers lightly touching. "And remember, please: Music is prayer."

We're rehearsing for the season's High Masses, Latin prayers like *O Salutaris* and *Panis Angelicus* and *Ave Maria* and varying arrangements of the *Tantum Ergo*. Though Sister Louise tosses Pope John a few crumbs like "Holy God We Praise Thy Name," we remain among the last congregants in the country to succumb to the retooled protocols of Vatican II. It seems that every new thing in America comes late to our town: rock-and-roll, collective bargaining, vinyl siding, the English-language Mass.

But the news of the president reaches us fast, the same way it reaches everyone: Somebody hears the radio, turns on the TV, calls everyone she knows. I'm lined up with the rest of the fifth-graders in the side lot after recess, waiting to return to our steam-heated classroom. Directly across the street—up there, top floor, behind the white sheers on the front-room windows—Denise's mother gapes at the

unfolding news. Perhaps she rushes to the window, looking for Denise and me, the two of us together in line as
always, the sky over our heads exceptionally high and bright
and cold. We've been on the girls' side, jumping rope on
bare pavement, the boys corralled on the boys' side, stran-
gling each other or hurling insults or hacking each other
with sticks. No snow to speak of yet and we're only six days
from Thanksgiving. I entertain myself by imagining everybody standing here next week, their teeth rattling in the first
snow, while I'm in Our Nation's Capital, walking into the
White House on the arm of my uncle.

Just beyond the flat rooftop of Denise's block, you can see
the windows of our parlor, where Mum, too, drops to a seat
in front of the TV and places her hand on her heart.

All at once, Sister Bernadette bursts from the building,
her small eyes rodent-red with turmoil. "Children," she begins. "A terrible thing has happened." Her doughy wrists jut
from her cuffs and she hugs herself. She's forgotten her coat,
a tiered woolen monstrosity that weighs thirty pounds. Her
mouth opens to the cold.

Oh, no.

Waiting in the crackled November sunshine, I can think
of only one Terrible Thing. My body feels like a river in the
act of freezing.

On the other side of the building, the third-graders in line
after their own recess, Sister Louise whispers something to
Sister Mary of Jesus, who blanches while Sister Louise faces
the line and says, "Children, I have very bad news." Betty
waits, docile and unmoved; everything about school is bad
news to her. But Cathy, who writes letters to Mum when
she's supposed to be practicing her times-threes or teaching
Betty how to knit, jumps to the same numbing conclusion:
Mum died.

But it's not Mum.

"Who?" I whisper to Denise. "Who did she say?"

First I don't hear, then I do. It's President Kennedy, Mum's other man. He has been shot.

"The president's dead, the president's dead!" shouts a kid in line, one of the histrionic boys. "There's gonna be a war!"

Who cares? Cathy and I are possibly the only two citizens of the United States of America who receive the heart-jangling, era-shaping news of twelve-thirty P.M., Central Standard Time, November 22, 1963, with a gulping wallop of relief.

Mum is home, making a salmon loaf for our no-meat Friday supper, alive alive alive.

New word: *assassination*.

Such a clamor, coast to coast, strangers from Detroit and Los Angeles and Hartford and New York sobbing into fuzzy microphones to tell the newsmen *I can't believe it, oh dear God, I can't believe it, how can we go on?* Mexico, too, mourns hard, especially the mothers, and most especially the Catholic mothers, who love beautiful Catholic Jackie even more than handsome Catholic Jack. Our First Lady wears boxy jackets with three-quarter sleeves. She sculpts her hair into shiny pageboys. She waltzes like a breeze-ruffled lilac. She rides brawny, upper-crust horses. Slim and graceful and humbly rich, she makes our mothers, in their cakelike hats from the fifties with fake flowers and crinkly veils, look suddenly dowdy and wanting. Jackie speaks "Paris" French, not the country French of our Franco neighbors. Her very name, *Jacqueline Bouvier*, honeyed and Continental, soaks our mothers with yearning.

Mum's 1963 Easter hat looked a lot like her 1962 Easter hat, but she'd come home from Doris's Dress Shop calling it a pillbox because that's what Jackie wore. "I like how it covers the head," she said, "but not the hair." This is what somebody on TV had said. Dad thought it a "desperate-handsome rig" for its trim of silk flowers. A month after that, she wore it to Dad's funeral.

And now Jackie, too, has suffered the unthinkable, her husband gone *like that.*

Jackie in her bloody pink suit.

Jackie with her children tucked close.

Jackie taking her brother-in-law Bobby's hand.

Jackie with her finishing-school posture, her high-born cheekbones, her bravery and poise.

Jackie bearing up.

In a different year Mum might have done like the other mothers, who are meeting at grocery counters to buy the Friday fish and break into tears. Instead, Mum stays home, watching the televised spectacle with a ferocious, private empathy. She, too, knows about bearing up. She'd followed her own husband's casket out of a church fogged with incense, her own mild brown eyes wounded and dry, her own coat buttoned up just so, as if to show everyone—even Jackie, had she been watching—how these things were done. She had her own little Caroline—three of them; her own Bobby; her own bravery and poise.

Our TV, like everyone's, stays on for three solid days while shock follows shock:

Walter Cronkite, our trustworthy newsman, breaking down on air.

Jackie getting off the plane, twenty-four hours since bang-shock-bang, still wearing the trim pink suit, its bodice defaced with blood and brain.

Another murder, on live TV, a shady character named

Jack Ruby gunning down the president's killer as he's led from a holding room by detectives wearing fedoras like Father Bob's.

Mum, who's refused us a Barbie for her "vulgar" proportions, lets us watch all this. She had shielded us from much of Dad's own Catholic goodbye, but we watch every second of the gruesome coverage, every second of the national wake, the national funeral, the national burial. Protecting us now from the death of a husband and father would be pretty much a locking-the-barn-door affair. The set stays on; Mum keeps vigil with Jackie, narrating the First Widow's first hours: the shell-shocked wife, the heartsick mother, the chin-up architect of the national funeral.

"Oh, girls. Look at that suit. That's blood."

"See that, girls? See how she's staring at nothing? She's thinking of the children now."

"She hasn't even changed her clothes. That's shock, girls."

"Mother of Mary, how is she ever going to tell them?"

"There she is, girls, God love her soul. Even in shock, how beautiful."

On and on, for three days.

"Look, girls, there's Bobby." The president's younger brother. His favorite. Caroline's uncle. "He'll be the man of the house now." She speaks with the quiet passion of an insider, her every observation delivered with a weary, unwanted authority.

"Bobby won't leave her side," she goes on, mopping her eyes. "Thank God she has him."

We watch it all: The president's casket with its crisp, distressing flag. Weeping citizens filing past in their cloth coats and fogged-up eyeglasses and homely shoes. Jackie and Caroline kneeling to kiss the casket.

Had we done that? Kissed Dad's casket?

Monday brings the president's funeral and burial, school closed, a national day of mourning. On Tuesday we'll leave for Baltimore and Our Nation's Capital, which is steeped in mourning; we'll miss school altogether this week, more time than we got for Dad.

"Look, girls, she's put her veil down now. She doesn't want people to see her face." The way she says it—*people*—makes me realize: other people. Not us. Because we know what's under there.

"Oh, those dear children. Little Caroline and John-John."

Our counterparts. I drink them in.

"She chose Arlington because the president was a war hero, girls. That's important—PT-109. Remember that."

We watch and watch: procession after procession, quiet but for the sound of horses' hooves and the heartbeat percussion of muffled drums.

New word: *caisson*. I toy with a memory of my making: Dad's trip to the cemetery, led by a riderless horse like Black Jack prancing and shying behind a six-white-horse-drawn caisson. I invent Dad's procession, Dad's twenty-one-gun salute, Dad's strangers from Detroit and Los Angeles and Hartford and New York keening into the cameras. Dad's widow, a veil covering the thing she won't let people see.

New word: *cortège*. Mum barely moves from the brocaded footstool, the closest seat to the TV. We watch the funeral cortège, stirred by the pomp and ceremony, the slither of low black cars, the sea of crosses at Arlington National Cemetery, and Black Jack with his polished hooves and nothing in his saddle but a pair of boots set backwards into the stirrups.

Symbolic, Anne says. The leader shall not ride again.

She sits on the couch with us, gathering us one-two-three. Mum gazes into the snowy light of the TV, her lips moving in prayer as she cries with Jackie. They could be sisters, conjoined in their loss.

"The eternal flame," Mum murmurs. "That was Jackie's idea. She's protecting his memory perpetually." That's what Mum had given Dad: "perpetual care." Which meant that St. John's Cemetery would keep the grass mowed for as long as the earth grew grass.

"It means forever," Mum adds, unnecessarily, since the word *perpetual* appears in all the prayers and half the hymns we've memorized since we were old enough to talk. "That flame will never, never be allowed to die, girls. That's how much she loved him."

Mum's empathy for Jackie swells her eyes, but beneath her sadness lies a profound relief, for she's harboring a secret she'll reveal only after we've returned safely from our trip. For two weeks now, her nighttimes have been plagued by the same vivid, persistent dream: three small, gaping holes in a graveyard.

What does this mean?

Dad's PEI lore had brimmed with ghosts and superstition, the usual ladies in gauzy nightgowns passing through the walls of snow-slumped farmhouses. Mum, too, had loved these stories and believed them wholly. And why not? One of Dad's nieces read auras and tea leaves, and Mum's eerie knack for attracting the devotion of animals had always struck us as a bequest from the Other Side. Plus, we were Catholic. If you believed that St. Juan Diego found fresh roses growing in winter, that St. Patrick told the snakes to leave Ireland *and they did*, that your nervous uncle could turn a wafer of unleavened bread into the literal body of Christ, then you were desperate well equipped for other kinds of magical thinking.

Mum had dreamed Dad's death and look what happened.

Now, days before taking to the highways in Aunt Rose's car, the haunting specter of those small open graves.

Front seat: the adults.

Back seat: Monnie, Cathy, Betty. One, two, three.

Do the math.

But over the weekend of November 22, the math suddenly adds up to a liberating, forehead-mopping relief.

One: the president.

Two: the killer.

Three: a Dallas police officer caught in the crossfire.

Awful about the president. Awful beyond telling. *We can't believe it, how can we go on?* But not as awful as the thing she thought God had in mind.

I'd heard only one other widow story by the time the president died, a story that began with a cousin of Mum's languishing with cancer. "C," people called it, fearing to bring the dreaded word into the house. They whispered its name as if it had ears, covered their mouths as if it had eyes. *The doctors opened him up, took one look, and closed him back up again.* This happened all the time, on both sides of the river, a secret sin on the soul of our valley, a grisly byproduct of the Oxford's bounty. Our viscous air and the mill below it; our fish-killed river and the mill above it: This was the great unmentionable, even when its eerie colors showed you the possibility of your own death. Because what your life received in return was worth the price.

Mum had taken us to visit Cousin Joe, a placid old man in his fluffy bed; his sweet, sorrowing wife, Jessie, brought in a plate of soda breads. She smoothed Cousin Joe's tiny bald head and his white, freckled hands.

A day later, the phone rang. Anne picked up, listened, turned to Mum. "Brace yourself," she said. This is what adults said: *Brace yourself.* Mum knew what was coming: Cousin Joe had died in the night.

"Brace yourself," Anne said again.

Again? Mum's eyes fired up; her soft hand moved to her heart.

"Jessie died half an hour later."

Dropped like Dad. A widow for thirty minutes, then mercifully killed by grief.

Lee Harvey Oswald created two widows that day, aside from his own: Jackie Kennedy and Marie Tippit, wife of J. D. Tippit, a patrolman with the Dallas Police Department. As Mum told and retold it, Marie got up at dawn to make her husband's breakfast, their three young children still abed. Officer Tippit's humdrum beat was Oak Cliff, a neighborhood of houses and swing sets and smiley dogs, but at thirty minutes past noon every cop radio in the city of Dallas crackled with instruction. Officer Tippit had just been home for lunch—Marie, again, a sandwich and fried potatoes—and with his full belly went on the lookout for a "thirty-year-old white male of slender build." He found one hurrying along East Tenth Street and guess who it was: the ferrety, slinking, pistol-packing murderer of our first Catholic president.

Officer Tippit slowed his cruiser, exchanged a few irrecoverable words with the slender male through the vent of the passenger-side window, then got out of the cruiser, where he was shot-shot-shot-shot in broad daylight before the pinned-open eyes of two bystanders. Three bullets to his powerful chest, one more to his handsome, beloved head. Shortly thereafter, Marie went the way of Jackie and Mum, a shuddering woman rocked by grief, looking into the eyes of her half-orphaned children.

Officer Tippit lived in a modest house and led a modest

life, a cop with two part-time jobs besides. His wife took in neighbor children to clink a few extra coins into the family till. They weren't much different from us, in fact: J. D. a little like Dad, Marie a little like Mum.

But when it comes to the art of emulation, it's Jackie Mum must choose, though she does not leave Mrs. Tippit unremembered. She'll spotlight every scrap of Tippit news that dribbles in over the coming weeks: a photo in *Life*, a sidebar in the *Lewiston Daily Sun*, a footnote in the TV retrospectives that begin appearing as soon as the smoke clears from the twenty-first saluting gun.

"Officer Tippit came home for lunch that day. Imagine, a normal lunch, a sandwich and fried potatoes. She had no idea."

"Jackie sent Mrs. Tippit a letter. 'We share a bond' is how she put it."

"The older boy came home sick with a bellyache. Pure coincidence that he saw his father one last time."

"The middle one's a girl."

"Jackie sent Mrs. Tippit a picture of the family. Not a posed one. A candid."

"He wasn't old enough for a pension, poor man."

And the *pièce de résistance:* "If it wasn't for FDR, Mrs. Tippit would be out scrubbing floors."

Jackie, for her part, after suffering in front of the whole world, plans to flee to a beach in Hyannis, sheltering her children from the press, nursing her private, serene, noble grief. She's right to leave Our Nation's Capital, Mum says, right to shun the press, right to hide her children. That family has suffered enough.

I don't know if I understood at the time what Mum was telling us—or even if she did—as she peeled back her own metaphorical black veil. I know I witnessed the return of her authority, her dignity, her willingness to turn her widow's face once again to the light. She never directly compared herself to Jackie, but often in the following months, standing at the stove, she might suddenly stop in mid-stir, cock her head like a bird, and say, "I wonder how she's making out." Never mind that the woman had more money than Moses and would in time break Mum's heart by marrying a Greek billionaire. For now, Jackie's story made Mum's bearable. *See?* she could have said, sitting under the dryer at Laura Remeika's beauty parlor, opening *Life* magazine's multipage spread of Jackie in her pink suit, Jackie on the tarmac, Jackie staring dead-eyed at the Bible while Lyndon Johnson takes the oath. *See? This is what widowhood looks like.* Of course she never said any such thing, but I believe she took a private comfort in the way Jackie had made grief look beautiful.

As we watch TV for three days straight, I observe my mother in a dawning wonder, having spent most of three seasons comparing my family to other families, both fictional and real. We're not the Vaillancourts with their working father, or the Gagnons with their fried toast and heaps of shoes. We're not the Marches of *Little Women*, with their grand piano and happy ending; or the Cuthberts of Green Gables, with their one irrepressible child; or the Drews, lousy with last-minute luck. We are, it turns out, bracingly closer to a family that seems equal parts real and make-believe: stoic and storied and rich, admired the whole world over. Imagine my surprise.

12

Our Nation's Capital

WE LEAVE MEXICO on Tuesday in sunlight, the president's death accompanying us like another passenger, not quite a relative but close. In the scant time she's had to shake off her three-graves dream and the drama of the cortège weekend, Mum's demeanor has both darkened and lightened simultaneously. A fervid urgency invades her sorrow. She rushes us into the back seat of her sister's car, hurry-hurry, as if thinking: *Hang on, Jackie dear. I'll be there before you know it.*

The downy flakes that meet us at the New Hampshire border thicken and stick and offer Aunt Rose's Chevy a woozy rapport with the road. My aunt inches along the interstate south of Boston as dusk comes upon us in the afternoon, Mum leading a rosary, Anne watching motel signs for a spot to duck from danger. NO VACANCY, they all say. NO VACANCY. Life feels mighty perilous in this week after assassination, and our world pulls a white blanket over itself to muffle the shock. Headlights and ambulance lights pulse off our windshield, and finally a lighted billboard at the highway exit, a quick decision, a fishtailing ride up a hill, and then a huge blinking VACANCY sign placed there, we know, by God Himself.

We get out into shin-deep snow. "You're a good driver, Rose," Mum says, shaking. This rare compliment between the sisters signals the obvious: We've had a narrow miss. Mum's dream was nearly right.

We blunder into a bright lobby, the adults relieved to spend money they never intended to spend. One room left and we take it. Two double beds, cots for the kids. Look, Cath, a mat in the bathtub! Little soaps you get to unwrap! Towel racks all over! A shower cap! (*I called it I called it I called it!*) An ice bucket? What's an ice bucket? Lookit lookit, Betty, the glasses have paper covers!

We've landed in Oz. Even Father Bob's rectory isn't fancy like this. We turn the shower on and off. Try on the shower cap. Watch a TV—Kennedy-Kennedy-Kennedy—with good reception. We take turns sitting on an unheard-of length of bathroom counter till Mum says that's enough. We yank the drapes back and forth, staring out at the snow-spun parking lot. We duck in and out, taking turns with the key, until Aunt Rose says quit it, right now.

The rest of this long evening—four-thirty and dark when we first pull out of the blizzard—fills with more firsts. The motel has an attached restaurant where we gorge on pancakes topped with whipped cream, a concoction we've never seen, not even in our excursions with Father Bob. Tonight's shaping up to be the best night of our life so far.

"Can we stay here tomorrow?" I ask, suddenly afraid of visiting the hospital. What if—? (*He's dead, isn't he?*) The fright of the highway exposes other, tucked-away worries.

"It'll let up," my aunt says, lighting a cigarette. We're back in our room, the lamps on. Aunt Rose sprawls on one of the beds, wiggling her stockinged feet. She whistles smoke through her lipsticky lips. At forty-three she already suffers a smoker's crosshatched face; she makes her own money and drives her own car and brings home snapshots from Credit Union conventions of herself in bright dresses, laughing harder than we ever see in real life, her arms draped over the high-laughing shoulders of other laughers. Aunt Rose was an infant in her cradle at the time of John James's death but nonetheless suffers her doomed family's worst consequence and manages through AA to keep stabbing the same unkillable dragon, the Irish curse. Through the years, and between the lines, I'll infer the humiliations that will precede her full redemption, but on this blizzardly night on our way to see Father Bob and possibly Jackie Kennedy, Aunt Rose is still my "nervous" aunt, tucked into bed with a cigarette between her lips.

"But what if it doesn't let up?"

"The worrywart," she says.

Betty, who can't read *Dick and Jane*, reads my down-deep fear: "IS FATHER BOB STILL THERE?"

"Of course," Anne assures us all. "He's fine. You'll see."

"He'll be glad to see you girls," Mum says. "Do him a world of good."

It takes a while to bed us down; we're too keyed up over our fancy digs. The adults stay up, rearranging our suitcases, laying out the next day's clothes. Then Aunt Rose turns in. Just before I drift off, I catch a snippet of conversation, Mum to Anne: "The problem is, he can't get over Dad."

Outside, the muffling snow falls in great, gorgeous, feathery layers. Is it snowing where he is? Weeks ago Father Bob sent us a treat: sock monkeys, the kind with red lips and cute red bottoms and long tails and little sock-monkey hats. Except mine wasn't a monkey, it was an elephant. Betty got a raccoon. Mum mailed him a card into which she tucked a photo of the three of us in front of the fridge, hugging our sock monkeys and holding a handmade THANK YOU sign.

Where did he buy these? we wanted to know. He went on car trips to faraway places and brought back T-shirts that said HOOVER DAM or LIBERTY BELL or ALAMO. He went all over the country, we thought, just to come home and open his softened road map and point here and there with the three of us crowding his light.

"He didn't buy them," Mum said. "He made them."

"HE MADE THEM?" Betty examined her raccoon in guileless wonder.

Cathy was impressed, too—she had the monkey, after all, the best one—but I got "nervous." What the heck kind of hospital taught you to make sock monkeys? I couldn't make sense of the image: Father Bob in his blacks—Father Bob who wove Walter Cronkite and *Sputnik* and Mister Ed the Talking Horse into his spellbinding Sunday homilies—trapped at a table with (I imagined) a bunch of beslippered *mémères*, his consecrated hands stuffing cotton batting into a monkey's cherry-red bum.

In my motel cot I'm visited by my own recurring dream, one that has plagued me since April: Fire! Our block on fire! Our things on fire! Our animals on fire! Help! Everything on fire!

I wince awake, convinced the motel room's ablaze, and indeed it is, an orange flickering reflection on the near wall. I lie there, paralyzed, eyes hitched open, mouth agape, unable to speak or scream or believe that nobody knows that our family is about to burn alive, and how will Father Bob get over *that*, when I turn over on my cot and through the window find the source of the fiery reflection: NO VACANCY. NO VACANCY. NO VACANCY.

"Behave," Mum warns us, as we get stiffly out of the car. Hangar-size parking lot zebra-striped with snow and black pavement and more cars than I've ever seen in one place, including at Lazarou's, Mexico's big car dealership. I don't remember being cold. We've dressed as if for church, our good outfits and Sunday shoes now slopped with wet.

In memory I ascend a thousand granite steps and a hospital lobby opens upward and outward, colorless and cavernous and full of plastic-smelling air. Mum goes up to a desk and asks something of a nun behind the glass. The hospital nuns wear white aprons and brutally starched wimples. These habits resemble those of the first nuns of my acquaintance, the Sisters of Mercy—the "Irish nuns"—at St. Athanasius in Rumford. We'd begun our parochial schooling there, boarding a bus at the Knights of Columbus hall every morning and riding to Franklin Street, two miles from French-nun St. Theresa's. St. A's had been Mum's first and best hope for Betty's Catholic education, something she and Dad had discussed endlessly with Father Bob.

Mum: Sister Stella Maris, she's especially interested in children like Betty.

Father Bob: Oh, yes. Yes indeed, she's made excellent *progress*.

But then came the hair-raising news: no more school bus from Mexico to Rumford. Dad left for work too early to drive us, so off we went in our new uniforms for our one-minute walk to the dreaded "French nuns" of St. Theresa's. Surprise: We already knew the required phrases, plus the full text of the Hail Mary (*Je vous salue, Marie, pleine de grâce . . .*), thanks to our having cleaved to Mrs. Gagnon's every mellifluous word.

At Irish St. A's I'd known a little boy named David who sledded into the killing path of a car. Black hair, white-white skin, snappy eyes, the best aloud-reader in my second-grade class, with a crystalline, clarifying voice. Sister Germaine herded us into church for the weekday funeral, a small casket as white and solid and uncrackable as a January freeze. Mum yelped with helpless anger when I came home and told her where I'd been, but she needn't have worried; at seven years old I didn't know the box had a boy in it. Sister's speech about death hadn't registered, so I drew my own conclusions. When David's mother floated into church in her half-buttoned winter coat and little veiled hat, I took her for a ghost; *someone* had died and I guessed it must have been her. Her bloodless face, her swollen eyes, a living person drained of life.

A shadow of that vision hovers as Father Bob appears—alive, but not in his blacks, inching down what seems now a massive, old-mansion staircase, the kind made for Grace Kelly's entrance in one of those romantic movies he loved.

It's him! It's really him!

Forgetting Mum's admonitions, we break into shrieks of joy and race each other to his arms. Cathy wins, Betty loses, and I remember my part in slow motion, noticing even as I thunder across the vast waxed floor how small he looks, how thin and lost, and I'm almost there, getting close, and where did he get that too-big bathrobe, almost there, and those ugly slippers, not the good ones we gave him last Christmas, almost there, his legs white and hairy and dead-looking, and I'm asking myself when did he make the sock monkeys, how did he make the sock monkeys, why did he make the sock monkeys, and then there I am in his arms.

First he cries. Then we do. Then a flutter in our periphery, people talking and not. Whispering and not. But we're inside a bubble called Father Bob and care not, for once, to overhear what adults are saying.

Mum and Aunt Rose and Anne close in then, and we huddle there, all of us. How small we must seem to the white-apron nun: this lost family, this frayed knot, this blot of Sunday-best color in the immense antiseptic hugeness of a Baltimore hospital for the Catholic and chronically nervous.

Time collapses after that. We're en route from the hospital to Our Nation's Capital, seven of us now sardined into Aunt Rose's car with the weather clear and clean and Father Bob at the wheel. Mum up front with her siblings; Anne in back with hers. Nobody singing the car-trip song. Cathy, the most reliable keeper of family memories, will recall nothing of this trip except for a low-grade anxiety, normally my territory. But I'm ten in this memory, and I believe that, like Nancy Drew, my obligation is to *crack the code, remain calm, decipher the clues*. It's not right that Father Bob has been stashed into this hospital-not-hospital, that they engaged him in the sad, dumb work of making sock monkeys instead of driving his car hither and yon and wowing his parishioners from the pulpit and visiting our classrooms in his blacks and collar and playing Scrabble with Mum and pinochle with us. How beautiful and terrible it had felt when we ran to him and he scooped us so hard to his breast.

Clue: Father Bob's been given permission—by whom? —to come with us in the car. Clue: He's been given permission—by whom?—to drive it himself. Or—big clue—he's been denied permission but insists on driving anyway.

I'm quiet for a time, sorting my info, and then, holy smoke! I remember.

Me: The president died! Fath, did you hear the president died?
Betty: HE GOT SHOT. THE MAN SHOT PRESIN-ENT KENNENY.
Yes, Father Bob says, I know. God rest his immortal soul.
Cathy: Officer Tippit, too, Fath. He got shot by the man, too.
Me: Lee Harvey Oswald. He lived in Russia!

Father Bob has cried over this, too, I can see. Why oh why did I mention it?

Then he makes a direction mistake, which never happens, and we're in a part of Our Nation's Capital that looks nothing like the postcards he himself once sent from here. No blooming, soap-bubble trees, no snow-clean monuments, no wide swept streets. Instead, lots of blocks that look sort of like ours but not really. Too many stacked stories, no yards, sidewalks garbagey and full of strange, not-garbage things. At the front of one set of stairs I spy something that looks like a shopping cart but can't be. The Norkuses would be steaming. NO TOO MUCH GARBAGE!

Everything in Washington is supposed to be white: the White House, the Capitol building, the monuments. Instead, black: black bunting hanging from narrow windows and shabby storefronts, the whole city draped in widow's weeds as we edge through these blackish streets that are the wrong streets.

"Are we lost?"

"Lock your doors, girls."

Uh-oh.

Father Bob puts his collar on.

Cars: black. Bunting: black. *People:* black! Until now I've never once beheld a black person. Not even one. Not any-where.

"Stop staring, girls."

We inch through an intersection, turn this way: black black black. Another intersection, this other way: black black black.

"We're going to have to ask somebody," Aunt Rose says. Father Bob keeps to the wheel, peering up at street signs. Clue: I've never seen him like this—lost. Lost in a car. This clue is even more confusing than black-black-black.

Finally Mum rolls down her window and Father Bob slows to a trembling stop.

"We're looking for the White House."

A black man in a puffy jacket peers in at us, whitest teeth I've ever seen. The whites of his eyes, too, look really white, the inside of his lip the baby pink of Mrs. Norkus's petunias. He takes our measure—what can he be thinking, a priest traveling with all these women? He smiles, points, gives Mum a set of quick, easy instructions. From the back seat we three gape at him with our mouths half open. Anne pats my knee: *Stop staring, sweetie.*

The puffy-coat man stands back after giving his big-smile directions: "Ya can't miss it!"

Mum will chuckle over this the whole day, repeating "'Ya can't miss it!'" as if to say, *Mother of Mary, they talk just like us!* She'll shake her head. "That man was so *nice.* Wasn't that man *nice,* girls? 'Ya can't miss it!'"

And we don't. Down this street, turn here, up that street, turn there, and look-girls-look: the White House, just where that nice man said.

Except we can't get near enough. Everything cordoned

off. No visitors. Pennsylvania Avenue feels quiet, deadened by what has befallen us all. We will not go to the White House after all; we will not, while being escorted through the grand rooms with the rest of the tourists, be spotted by Jackie herself; the First Widow will not suddenly open a door and slip into view and lock eyes with Mum and say, "We share a bond." It occurs to the adults, belatedly, that Jackie might not even be there. She might already have taken the children to Hyannis. "Good," Mum says, nodding. "Good for her."

Up and down the somber streets, we take in the sights in silence. Past one massive monument after another, circle upon circle, an aimless vigil. I don't understand that Father Bob is sick, and in despair, and drying out, and scared, but I know enough to be awed that he manages to do here what he does everywhere: drive. Today is Thanksgiving but nothing Thanksgiving-ish survives this memory of driving.

We drive past white columns and white domes and statues of colossal white men on white horses, but Father Bob passes them all without comment because he's looking for the basilica of the Immaculate Conception, the largest Catholic church in North America, which he can't find. We wind up—clue: by accident—in a neighborhood of pretty brick houses sheltered by black iron gates. We drive and drive, down one narrow street and up another, ogling the houses' tall windows, their slate roofs and granite steps and handsome doors. Then, more streets in this mourning city, more turns, stop someplace for lunch, sandwiches oddly stabbed with frilly toothpicks and gross green olives, then more streets, and a highway, and then *Here we are, girls*, alarmingly, back in the parking lot of the sock-monkey hospital.

Us: What—?

Aunt Rose: Time to go home.

Anne: It's all right, girls. He'll be back before you know it.

Father Bob: I'll be back before you can shake a stick.

"Before you can shake a stick" means a long time. We're young enough, and old enough, to know at least that. Now we're boo-hooing, digging in. A white-apron nun comes flapping across the lot. Father Bob gets out. His eyes water up; his cheeks have disappeared, two flat, chalky panes of skin in their place.

HE'S NOT COMING?

Not yet, hon.

What do they mean, he's not coming? Isn't this why we drove down here? Isn't this why we stayed at that motel in a blizzard? Isn't this why why why can't he come back home?

Because.

Pleeeease!

Come, girls, in the car.

Pleasepleaseplease!

In the car, girlsies! Come on, quick! Quick like a bunny!

We kiss him and hug him—*Bye, Fath! Bye, Fath!*—and get in the car and head back north through what I remember now as a miraculous tunnel of sunny weather like the parted seas of Moses: storms on either side, coastal storms sweeping out to sea, western storms petering out in Ohio. We pull into a Howard Johnson's and slide into a big orange booth.

Mum looks over the menu, adjusting her glasses. She's wearing a good dress, her lipstick and perfume, her crystal earrings from Dad. Her hair falls in short cloudy waves. Mum frowns over the big print, pretending to decide, but really she's looking for something cheap. "I'll have the Tommy Tucker," she tells the waitress.

"That's a children's plate," the waitress says.

"Oh," Mum says. She blushes, because now the waitress knows.

"I'm not very hungry. It looked small."

"Children only."

So Mum orders a hamburger like the rest of us, her cheeks blazing. Is she thinking of Jackie with her bone china and embroidered linen? She starts to chuckle, because the Tommy Tucker sounds so funny, and now we're all laughing, even as I redden up myself on Mum's behalf.

Back in the car, we take turns saying, "I'll have the Tommy Tucker!" as the highway exits zip past.

"And here I was," Mum says, hooting now, "all dressed up! Can you imagine the waitress in the back, telling the cook, 'That woman ordered the Tommy Tucker, and she was wearing crystal earrings!'"

"I'll have the Tommy Tucker!"

"Ya can't miss it!"

Past the car windows, a thousand amazing things: oil tanks; water towers; trees full of long black birds; tall, tee-tering houses with peeling paint; highway signs and inter-changes; other cars crowded with kids, their parents in the front moving their lips. Who are they, these stranger chil-dren whom I count up, three here, five there, sometimes one lone face staring out of a back-seat window? Where are they going? I wonder. Where have they been?

In two days we arrive home—"made good time," as Fa-ther Bob would put it—where everything looks the same as when we left, because it is.

Looking back on that trip to Washington now—a breath-taking distance of forty-five years—I wonder: As Father Bob drove the narrow streets of Georgetown, looking for the great basilica in the wrong neighborhood, could I have glanced above the slate rooftops and spotted the imposing edifice of Healy Tower on the campus of Georgetown University? I hope I did; I like to think I caught a bright glimpse as I sat in the back seat of my aunt's burdened car, feeling throat-tight and afraid. I hadn't the faintest notion—how could I?—that I'd one day return to this city as a matriculated French major, a move engineered by Father Bob (*You can't go wrong with the Jesuits, Monnie*), whose jubilation at my acceptance would render him helpless with laughter, his old ho-ho-ho laugh by then long restored.

The memory begins like this: I'm waiting on the street in front of our block, Father Bob stuffing my suitcases into the trunk of his Barracuda, my heart already fisted and homesick. The street seems far down; or, our apartment seems far up, everything distorted, overbright, surreal.

The sun is vivid but cold. I become suddenly aware of myself as a beneficiary of gravity, feeling my tenuous connection to the earth. I can't say where exactly Earth is right now in relation to the sun—I barely passed physics but got into Georgetown anyway; from some perspective, somewhere in the universe, I must be standing upside down without feeling it. Father Bob shuts the trunk and says, *Well, Monnie, I guess it's time to shove off.*

Goodbye, Mum. Her body feels warm, as it always does. Cushiony as a feather tick, nearly nappable. But it's too late to sleep in my mother's embrace. I've been eighteen for two weeks; all grown-up. So I leave her there, on our street, the last glimpse I'll ever have of her whole.

Father Bob has bought my plane ticket and drives me to the Portland jetport, assuaging my terror by enthusing over the Jesuits' legendary reverence for learning, their worship of the intellect, their joy. He walks me all the way to the gate, kisses and hugs me. *Bye, Fath! Bye, Fath!*

At the other end of this knee-shaking odyssey, I land at D.C. National, follow the signs to baggage claim (Anne's written instructions), and wait for the conveyer to spit up my suitcases (soon I'll be calling them *bags*). In the patient, practiced crowd—am I the only one who's never done this?—I spot a man from home, the hound-faced, ludicrously tall Ed Muskie, our senator. He bends from his great height to pick up his own bag, which—by design?—comes first off the belt. *Hello, I'm from Mexico,* I practice to myself. *Hello, Senator, my mother was in your class.* Before I can will myself to approach him, another passenger grabs my place, engaging him in vigorous discussion, probably about the Clean Water Act, which the senator has been constructing law by law, amendment by amendment. *All these regulations,* the Maine voter is probably saying. *We can't compete.* Same thing everybody says. *Leave the water alone.*

When the Maine voter turns away, I try to catch the senator's eye, hoping he'll recognize me as a Mexico girl. But I don't look much like a Mexico girl, in my new pixie haircut and the traveling outfit Anne picked out and Mum approved: paisley polyester "dress shorts" and a matching blouse. I wear them with pantyhose and white sandals. *Excuse me, Senator,* I say again to myself, but the senator vanishes into a jostle of strangers. I follow a sign for "ground transportation," which I'd have taken for directions to a sidewalk if not for Anne's instructions.

The taxi driver is a black man who reminds me of that long-ago trip to Our Nation's Capital, our somber ride through the draped streets. Might I work "Ya can't miss it!" into our conversation, make him chuckle the way the puffy-coat man made my mother chuckle? As I open the door, he looks up crossly, says something I can't catch.

"Excuse me?" I ask, holding the door open. My heart is killing me.

"In the back."

"In the—?" I keep my hand on the front-door handle, glancing fearfully into the back seat.

"In the *back*," he repeats. He glares into my ignorant freckled face. "Sit in the back."

My eyes heat up; I scramble into the back seat, smoothing out my shorts, holding my new purse from Doris's Dress Shop, trying not to cry. At home, if you had to take a taxi, you sat in the front, with the driver—common courtesy. Then the driver asked you how was school.

It takes a long time to get to campus and at the end the man charges me twelve dollars—which I pay, plus one dollar extra (also on Anne's instructions). Weeks later, comparing notes with my streetwise roommate, I'll discover his trick, Georgetown via the wrong bridge, many extra miles, my punishment for trying to sit up front. For being polite. For trying not to appear uppity.

He drops me at a dorm swarming with girls arriving from New York and Chicago and Boston and Philadelphia, their parents lugging televisions and stereos and trunks packed with new bedspreads and beaded curtains and posters of Cat Stevens. In minutes I come to understand how unhip I look, dragging my hometown behind me like a shirttail I can't keep tucked in. When two boys—you'd have to call them men; older, bearded premed students—dart from the lobby to help me with my things, I'm struck dumb with fear. If only Denise were here, but she's in Worcester, Massachusetts, moving into a dorm at Assumption College, a place where kids like us belong.

That first day on my own will last nearly all night, all

the moving in and signing up and meeting girls with ankle bracelets and boys with shoulder-length curls. Ann from Chicago and Mindy from Pittsburgh and Jamie from Baltimore; Rob from Philly and Dan from Louisville and Andy from Altoona. My roommate is Christine from Trenton, being moved in by her brother, Saul, whose name I ask for again, thinking he's said "Salt." My stupendous ignorance being revealed by the minute, I encounter food I've never eaten (I take the Cobb salad in the cafeteria, believing the hairnetted lady has mispronounced *crab*), places I've never heard of (Grosse Point; the Upper East Side; the Mainline), and cursing I've never heard in such electrifying ubiquity (fuck this fuck that fuck everything). I walk the campus with a sweaty map, classroom buildings spilling outside the stone walls into the streets, where I glance up alleyways for possible rapists. Then a party in the quad, where Mike from Levittown wheedles me into a date and I say yes even though I mean no, and I come back to my room—first key I've ever owned—to find it filled with kids and beer, so I sit there, cross my naked legs (pantyhose are laughable, I've learned since morning), and join a mortifying, elliptical conversation in which it must be explained to me, in patronizing enunciations, that Greenberg is a Jewish name, whereupon I must admit that I have never met a Jew. A Bernstein from Brooklyn turns to me in abject, half-admiring wonder and asks: "Where the fuck are you *from*?"

He laughs. He calls me the girl from Spain, Maine. He forgives me. They all forgive me. And by Halloween Eve, richly befriended, I return to my dorm from a class called The Problem of God (that's the Jesuits for you), alight with teachers who thrill me and ideas that shock me and plans that include Paris—the city in Europe, not the town back home in Maine. I shuffle my happy burden of books to one arm, unlock the door with my first key, and rush inside to grab my ringing phone.

It's Anne, who says, "Brace yourself."

By then, Father Bob will have become the man who can meet me at the Portland jetport and hold back his tears to make room for mine. The man into whose arms I will run, run, run like a girl, though I fancy myself a woman after two months away. The man who, as I stagger to the car, will hold me up as he must, his drinking done with, his nervous period behind him. The man who, on the drive back to Mexico, will calmly be able to repeat the unrepeatable: Mum has cancer; they operated two days ago; last night she had a rare, unforetold, massive, postsurgical stroke.

I ask and listen, ask and listen, and his voice does not falter. Mum's much-loved face is now a lopsided puzzle, her entire left side immobilized, her speech a confusing garble. One hand on the wheel, the other holding mine, my uncle will be the man who can lay out these unfaceable facts and face them. For the whole of Mum's ordeal—the cancer will return in short order and take her for good—he will be that man.

That's the man he will become, but today, two days after Thanksgiving of 1963, as Aunt Rose drops us off and we trundle over the slushy driveway and tromp back upstairs, I have no inkling of this, or any, future. I know only that we've left Father Bob in the sock-monkey hospital, that the whole country is in shock after what happened to the president, and that a tiny, colorful fragment of Mum's spirit has magically reappeared. I check her purse for my souvenirs—a cardboard coaster from a Howard Johnson's and a plastic replica of the Washington Monument—and there they are, safely transported, just as she promised.

On Sunday night—Mum unpacking our things after the trip to Our Nation's Capital, the washing machine thrashing and bumping in the bathroom—the past few days already seem like a dream. I imagine Father Bob back in his room at the sock-monkey hospital, gazing out at the parking lot, maybe looking for us even though he saw us leave with his own eyes, even though he knows that by now we've made it all the way back home.

As Anne helps us lay out our school uniforms for the following morning, the phone rings. It's Sister Mary of Jesus, suggesting to Mum that Betty might be "happier at home."

Would she ever.

Mum goes quiet, but her bearing is newly chin-up, Jackie-like. She nods into the phone, listening. "Yes, Sister," she says. "I've thought of that." She squints at the ceiling, pretending to be weighing the pros and cons, but she's been mulling the same handful of facts for years. She knows.

"Thank you, Sister," she says. "I'll think about it, Sister."

Come morning, Cathy and I leave our Pupil behind forever. Oh, that lucky duck. We feel jealous but strangely heartsick, we three now we two. Two girls walking down the street every morning. Two sets of uniforms draped over the ironing board.

That night, in bed, Cathy and I converse quietly, almost reverently, in a mélange of regular English and a language we made up when we first learned to talk. Like certain Eastern tongues to which we've never been exposed, our communication depends on pitch and stress for meaning. Only one example from the lexicon has been cleared for public scrutiny:

Ecana egala (*ee-CAH-na ee-GAH-la*): 1. Exclamation of self-regard, e.g., *"Aren't we something else!"* 2. Exclamation of dismay, e.g., *"Oh, shoot."* 3. Exclamation of affection, e.g., *"I love you so much, please don't die."*

In the dark, Betty listens. She understands our language, too, understands that we're both glad and not glad that Mum finally took her out of school. In the kitchen Mum and Anne murmur to each other over a cup of Red Rose tea. As their spoons clink, I pretend the sound is silver, that they've got a silver pot and bone-china cups out there, that Mum could be Jackie and Anne one of the young Kennedy women—maybe Teddy's wife—talking things over at the end of a day filled with long cars and candelabras.

Cathy drifts off, sounding like a soft-snoring mouse, whispery, babyish, disturbingly weak. Across the narrow gap, Betty in her bunk drifts off, too, in airy sighs of relief now that school's out for good. I remain pulsingly awake, suddenly haunted by the president's bloody death and the nuns' terror tales of the holy saints and martyrs dying six ways from Sunday: flayings and stabbings and lightning strikes and conflagrations at the stake and plain old *dying in their sleep*. For hours, it seems, I wait in wakeful vigil between my sleeping sisters, unnerved by the hitches in their little mouse breaths. When at last I succumb to the weight of my forced-open eyes, another breathing enters my conscious world, beyond our room, beyond our windows, beyond the reach of the holy saints and martyrs.

Puff . . . puff . . . oooom, it goes. *Puff . . . puff . . . oooom.*

It's the Oxford, over there on the riverbank, that faithful, heavy-breathing monster, the huff-and-puffer that glows in the dark. Dad no longer goes in there and out, but its potent self somehow abides, immense and inescapable, bigger than the rumors of change: cutbacks, reorganization, maybe a sale. *Puff . . . puff . . . oooom.* It never varies, this sound, this inhale and exhale, all day, all night, a mountainous, animal presence.

Cathy makes another mouse cry and startles awake. Betty, too, is stirring. *Shhh*, I whisper, *listen*. A brief, bright thought comes to me, fueled by the religious pageantry of the president's three-day funeral and our own secret brush with celebrity: Maybe Dad can speak to us through the steam.

We listen, all three, absorbing the sound as children from the coast might absorb the tidal sighing of a nearby sea, an ebb and flow so enduring that after a time the sound appears to be coming from within your own unsuspecting self. It's been a long seven months, April to November, a tender time bracketed by death. A father, a president; the one grieved only by us, the other by a whole spacious-sky, purple-mountains-majesty, grain-waving country. I listen, with my sisters, in a kind of stupefied surrender, as the mill's enduring breath smoothes over us, inhale, exhale.

After a while, it's clear enough, I know at last and for good: Dad's no longer in there. Or anywhere reachable. Dad is gone, Dad is gone, even as the sound of his life's work presses in, closing our heavy eyes. By the time Anne slips into our room, kisses our slackened faces, and crawls into her own bunk, we have all, one-two-three, gone sound asleep.

13

Anniversary

A ND THEN—HOW COULD this be?—another April,
1964, the Norkuses' crocuses popping through the
grass, a second springtime without Dad. For his anniversary Mass, we file into St. Theresa's church in our good
clothes, all of us praying side by side in the front pew, the
town outside the church windows seeming less and less like
the vibrant thing from which our father so suddenly vanished, taking all that vibrancy with him.

I open my hymnal, mouth the responsorial psalm, and
wonder: Would he remember me? I wear glasses now, blue
cat's-eyes like Mum's; I'm two and a half inches taller; my
hair, though still red like his, sweeps away from my face in a
big-girl "flip"; I'm in fifth grade going on sixth. Heaven, it
is said, brims with God and music and other divine distractions. If he came back and I said, *Hi, Daddy*, would he know
it was me?

How has one year—a year containing almost everything

I will ever know—passed so invisibly? Twelve months have melted behind me like snow.

"Why, look, children!" squeals Sister Bernadette, setting down her flash cards. She loves flash cards, uses them for French, English, History, Math. "Look who's here!"

"Bonjooour, mon Père!"

Back at work since the first of the year, Father Bob has edged once again into the waking world. I'm the only one here who knows where he's been. He jaunts into our classroom, cassock riffling at his heels, still trying hard but less gutted by the effort. Since his sojourn at the sock-monkey hospital—*I had a very good doctor* is all he'll ever say—my uncle has recovered the dropped notes in his layered voice. "Boys and girls," he says, arms akimbo. "What's *nyew?*"

Sister Bernadette, a terrible singer, has nonetheless taught us seven songs, one for every sacrament. We treat Father Bob to a rendition of "Holy Orders Made It So" as he nods along, smiling beneath the portrait of President Kennedy that Sister has not deigned to remove. Like the whole country, we've grown grudgingly used to the new president, Mr. Johnson, with his boring, Protestant, not-cute, too-old daughters; and his big-hair wife who goes by the silly name of Lady Bird.

"Very pleasant," Father Bob says to us, applauding. "Very, very pleasant." His smile looks more like his real smile, his cheeks pink with health, his forehead clear. "Denise Vaillancourt, how are your mother and father?"

"They're fine, Father. Thank you, Father."

"And Margie Lavorgna, your mother's still working at Larry's?"

"Yes, Father. Thank you, Father."

My uncle gives me his special glance—*I know you're*

here—and I all but slurp it up. My heart aches, in a good way. This man standing before us wouldn't be caught dead stuffing a sock monkey.

"Thank you, Sister."

"Oh, thank *you*, Father!"

"Au revoir, mes enfants."

"Au revoir et merci, mon Père!"

Before he leaves, he prepares to bless us. He asks us to think of our families, the better for his blessing to extend its reach. He knows, in a way that we children cannot, that the ground beneath Mexico's mothers and fathers has begun to quaver. Something new has moved to town: *efficiency*—competition's heartless sidekick. A nearby shoe shop closing for good, the entire Maine shoe industry teetering on collapse. At the mill, another bumpy season of labor negotiations lies just ahead, stepped-up rumors jangling everyone's nerves as our competitors—foreign and very, very efficient—load cheaper paper onto ships and planes, towers of paper destined for American trucks and trains that will convey the goods to stationery stores and pressrooms and insurance companies and publishing houses from sea to shining sea.

Father Bob raises his hand for the blessing. He looks older, seems older. Not only him. Me. All of us. The whole country. Everyone and everything touched by death.

"In nomine Patris, . . ." Father Bob says.

Down go our heads. I think of my family, as Father Bob asked. Anne at the high school teaching Shakespeare; Cathy at her desk in the classroom downstairs from me, learning her times-fives from Sister Mary of Jesus; Betty at home drawing snowmen with Mum. Her fling with Jackie Kennedy worked magic on us children; maybe that was the point all along. I no longer cry every night over Dad, and if someone asks me, "Who's your father?"—as people do back then—I can look that stranger in the eye and say "deceased" and know that we both hear the tacit postscript: *Just like Caroline's father, our assassinated president.*

The *Times:* OXFORD PAPER COMPANY EARNINGS UNCERTAIN.

One Monday during that anniversary spring, I come home from school to find my brother in the kitchen drinking coffee with Mum. I rarely see him like this—alone, without his wife and kids—and never on a workday.

I put down my books. "Did something happen?" I glance frantically around. There's Betty in Dad's chair, listening. Cathy, I know, is a few paces behind me, walking home with one of the Gagnon girls. Is it Anne? Father Bob? Cumpy or Aunt Rose? Who is it? Who?

Barry says something about a wildcat. I picture a big animal doing something bad.

"What? What did you say?"

A wildcat walkout. This morning at the Oxford, fourteen machine tenders left their posts in protest over the first occurrence of job combining, which sounds like *including* but really means *excluding*. In job combining (Mr. Vaillancourt says) you get assigned to two machines on a single shift, dashing from, say, the rewinder to the supercalender and back, cutting two crews by half a man.

Subtracting one job by *adding* yourself to two jobs. A human antonym. Nobody wants to be that man.

By noon word spread to every sector of the mill, from the beater room to the woodyard, and the place emptied out. Almost nobody went in for second shift. The union scheduled an emergency meeting for tonight, which is why Barry is here drinking coffee and talking to Mum.

"He loved that place," Mum says, shaking her head. "The man practically *lived* there."

Barry says to her, "Well, he wouldn't recognize it now."

What's going on? Aren't we the Oxford? The mighty, mighty Oxford?

"Guys are mad as hell," Barry says to Mum. "They mean business."

The walkout ends on Wednesday morning, two days later, but a tone on both sides has been brazenly set. Contract talks will begin soon; our town is in for a long summer.

The *Times:* THREE OXFORD WORKERS FIRED AFTER WILD-CAT WALKOUT; ELEVEN SUSPENDED.

Shortly after school lets out for the summer, mill manager Charles Ferguson publishes an open letter in the *Times* to the citizens of Rumford and Mexico, pleading that a strike *will serve no purpose whatever. In addition to depriving you of your pay,* he reminds one and all, *it would hamper the company's ability to satisfy the needs of its customers. Without customers, the Company is out of business and your job security disappears. The rumor of a work stoppage may be without foundation, but I felt that you should know the facts before it's too late.*

The facts: We are the Oxford. The mighty, mighty Oxford. *National Geographic* loves us, they buy only Oxford paper for their color-picture magazine, which you can find all over town—all over America! all over the world!—stashed into bathroom magazine racks, towered onto parlor tables, stacked against screen doors to keep them from slamming shut. That's *our* paper on which you read articles about African matriarchies and babies born at the North Pole and flowers so small and rare you can't find them without a magnifying glass. That's *our* paper in a magazine so colorful they pile up like totems because no mother in America—or the world!—can bear to throw one out.

The *Times:* BUILDING CAMPAIGN CONTINUES AT OX-FORD.

The *Times:* OXFORD EARNINGS DROP.

The facts: Charles Ferguson came to our door, fifteen months ago now, to say, *I'm sorry for your loss.* He put on a jacket and took Mum's hand and said kind words because Dad was a foreman in the woodyard, a good worker who was never late, a member of the long-service club, part of the Oxford family. Charles Ferguson—someone *important,* someone *up there*—ascended our stairs, past the Norkuses', past the Hickeys', and came to us, his Oxford Paper Company pin glinting on his lapel.

The *Times:* UPP WINS AGAIN; NEGOTIATIONS SET FOR AUGUST 3.

The *Times:* NEGOTIATIONS BEGIN.

The *Times* follows the zigzagging road of compromise, one edgy meeting after another. It follows also our hum-drum daily doings. In one issue I learn that Chief Maurice Cray brought a complaint "against a Rumford citizen" who illegally parked in Mexico; that the sensational Impacts are back at the Eagles hall; that a Rumford meteorologist pre-dicted a colder-than-normal autumn ("*So sorry . . . signed, Armand A. Violette*"). Senator Muskie publishes a defense of the Clean Water Act on page three. And on the next page, an anonymous essay called "The Truth about Cancer," lament-ing the Hollywood deaths of Charles Laughton and Dick Powell. "They have not died in vain," proclaims the mysteri-ous scribe who lauds the release of the dirty word *cancer* into polite company.

On the facing page, a reporter's note on the specs of the

Oxford's new grinding room: Made of concrete. Covered with asbestos felt. No windows.

The *Times:* NEGOTIATIONS CONTINUE.

The *Times:* MANAGEMENT SPIKES RUMORS OF WHOLE-SALE PERSONNEL CHANGES.

The *Times:* BOTH SIDES LESSENING DEMANDS.

The *Times:* NEGOTIATIONS STALLED AT OXFORD.

During the mid-August labor talks, Denise and I celebrate our eleventh birthdays, five days apart, a cake for me at her house, a cake for her at my house. In celebration, I decide once and for all to rectify the Vaillancourts' only perceptible deficiency by smuggling into Denise's bedroom a homeless yellow cat we pick up on Gleason Street. The cat will live in the closet and be fed in secret until we can soften up Denise's parents by inventing the cat's dramatic backstory, in carefully timed, increasingly theatrical installments, salting it with quotes from St. Francis, the patron saint of animals ("O Divine Master, grant that I may not so much seek to be consoled, as to console"), until finally Mrs. Vaillancourt, wracked with guilt, will mutter, *Jesus Mary and Joseph, you girls are right as always, let us open wide our doors!*—whereupon we cue the cat for his big reveal.

Denise has a blabby little brother, however; before we can pass a single afternoon with our yellow birthday cat, Mr. Vaillancourt appears, filling the doorway of the bedroom with his square, stern shoulders and disciplinarian face. He's just come back from a union meeting. Is he mad about the cat (at the moment unraveling an afghan crocheted by an auntie or *mémère*) or mad about NEGOTIATIONS STALLED?

"What do you girls think you're doing?"

His eyes are pond blue, like Dad's. Twinkly. He reminds

me of a tame bear. I pick up the cat, who is purring beatifically, an ambassador from St. Francis for sure. It has a well-brushed coat and clean, translucent ears and come to think of it might not actually be homeless. I shift its fetching visage so that Mr. Vaillancourt can better admire its beseeching, topaz-colored eyes.

"We're sorry, Dad," says Denise, whose negotiation skills are just plain pitiful.

To this lame defense I must add, prematurely, our trump card: "We named him Omer."

I remember Mr. Vaillancourt's laugh as a modest, rolling chuckle, as if he disliked making too much of himself. This pleasant, trickling sound trails him like fairy dust as he trots downstairs—without a word of reproach—and sets the cat outside.

"Mr. Vaillancourt?" I ask when he returns. "Are you mad at me?"

He shakes his head no; he's not mad at me. In time I'll come to understand that I break his heart. He pats my head. He looks me in the eye. He calls me dear. He asks me how's your mother. Then he goes to the phone, for he's been called in, again, to do battle with a monstrous machine.

The *Times:* DEADLOCKED.

How strange it seems to be leaving town with a strike looming, everyone coiled tight. But that's exactly what we're doing, leaving town. Father Bob has a one-week vacation and has invited us all on a trip in his new Impala: he and Mum and Anne in front, we three girls in back, a long car trip with restaurants and everything. He's so much better now, his stay at the hospital now nine months old. On a hot morning in late August, he drives us out of town via Route 2, passing the Rumford falls and heading for the falls at Niagara, a journey that echoes in reverse the one taken by our industrial founder.

In Niagara Falls—the Canadian side—we check into a motel called the Empress and feel like royalty.

"Lookit, Cath! Lookit, Bet! A swimming pool!"

Indeed: a long blue pool ringed by large, painted climbable wooden animals, a fantastical mirage shimmering under high soft lights. It's too late to swim, but Mum and Anne allow us to try out the animals while they perch at one of the plastic poolside tables and Father Bob goes inside to pay. Already this is nothing like our other trip; it hasn't occurred to me even once to try to listen between the lines. All I want is to climb to the top of the elephant—there are steps built into its back—and holler, "Hellooo, down there!"

In the morning, Father Bob bangs on our door. "Get up, girls! The day's half gone!"

Mum comes out of the bathroom, her hair still in pin curls. "For crying out gently, Father," she tells her brother, "it's only seven o'clock."

But Father wants to *shove off*, he wants to *get this train moving*, especially since his derailment at the sock-monkey hospital. He means to fulfill his duty as small-*f* father twice over if he can manage it, making up for lost time, cramming all the small-*f* fathering he can stand into his one-week vacation. So we wash our faces and find our bathing suits and gather like cats waiting for the door to open.

"Now! Now! Now!"

But it turns out that Father Bob begins every day of his priestly life with morning Mass, no exceptions. He walks in wearing not his plaid swimming trunks but his cassock and surplice. Mum clears the motel dresser of feminine clutter as

Father Bob lays out a makeshift Mass: portable paten, portable linens, portable tin holding a stash of unconsecrated hosts.

Cathy and I swap a look. *"Ecana egala,"* she whispers, which does not, in this case, mean *I love you*. It means *Oh, shoot*.

We fall groaningly to our knees on the motel carpet as Father Bob murmurs the Offertory, consecrates six hosts, and administers Communion first to himself, then to us, in order of age: Mum, Anne, Betty, me, Cathy. With a pool shimmering just outside the window, this quickie Mass becomes the offer-up of all offer-ups.

"Amen!" we cry, then we shove off, we get this train moving, breakfast in the motel restaurant, which—*holy smoke!*—serves the same whipped-cream-on-pancakes as that other motel. Then an hour in the pool—*heave ho! heave ho!*—after which Father Bob hurries us down to the lookout or to the arcade or to the museums or to the hot-dog stands, the falls' presence tremoring beneath us no matter where we walk. He herds us to gardens with words spelled out in flowers, pays our way into an animal show where a portly green parrot rides a red bicycle and sings "O Canada." He takes us to the Ferris wheel, the cotton-candy kiosk, and the merry-go-round, which is too sissy-baby but Betty likes it and won't ride alone. Lunch at a place where they sprinkle vinegar on the French fries. Back at the motel we climb on the giant wooden animals and cannonball straight into the safety net Father Bob makes of his arms. Over and over and over.

Eventually, we swim to the side of the pool—Betty with her blow-up tube—tired now, and quieting. Before lifting us to the deck, where we can pad back to Mum and Anne,

Father Bob confides to us, "Your mother will never get married again. You know that, right?"

This seeming non sequitur splashes softly down, a perfect landing. He's read our minds—might some cheap substitute, some other man, start up Dad's car one day?—and now our minds have been set at permanent ease.

"Are you having fun, girls?" Anne calls from a chaise longue, her face damp from the pool. Mum, too, has tried the water, her feet still bare.

"Yes!" we yell. "We're having fun!" We mean it.

At midweek Father Bob springs for a river tour of the falls, where the boat man punches our tickets and winks at Anne and hands out oversize slickers. My bangs and eyelashes beaded with river mist, I wince against the concussive roar of the falls. You could run a hundred paper mills on the strength of that roar, raise up a hundred towns, produce paper enough for all the books in America. But I see no smokestacks, I hear no mill whistles; instead, I stand with my family and gape at the plummeting water, feeling the way Hugh J. Chisholm must have felt at his first glimpse of the Rumford falls.

"Wow," Mum says, swiping at her hair. "That was something." We're wet, all of us, shedding the soaked slickers. Between the swimming pool and the falls, we'll be wet every day—a metaphorical cleansing made literal. The adults seem lighter, looser, cleaner in spirit, beautiful with water—water, not tears—dripping off their eyelashes. In a few days I'll be parked at a sixth-grade desk, stiff-backed in my itchy skirt and overstarched blouse, learning the rules of a different nun for a different grade; but for now I am staring into the thunder of waterfalls, shaking water off the ends of my fingers. Despite the shuddering of the falls beneath its surface, the ground, for the first time since Dad died, has ceased to shift.

"Well, girls, it's our last day," Father Bob says. He's packed up his portable Mass and bought breakfast and now we're standing outside the motel restaurant looking down the hill toward the falls. "What do you want to do? Pick anything."

"I think Mum should pick," Anne says. "What do you say, girls?"

"Mum should pick! Mum should pick!"

Father Bob laughs. "Okay, Margaret. You pick."

Mum looks sweet as an apple in her sky-pink dress, her white shoes. "I wouldn't mind going back to the arcade," she says. "And the wax museum."

"Yaaay!"

At the arcade, where a buffet of distractions includes a shooting gallery, bumper cars, and a fortune-telling machine, Mum beelines for the barrel in which Mrs. Annie Taylor, a sixty-two-year-old schoolmarm, tumbled over the falls at the turn of the century in a desperate attempt to make herself rich and famous. She got half her wish: The display takes up a good chunk of floor space, giant placards relating the story of a life that ended in a pauper's grave.

Mum lingers there, reading, studying a grainy, blown-up photograph of the dumpy little daredevil in her long skirt and high-neck blouse, already exhausted and battered-looking.

"Must've felt like the inside of an automatic dryer," Mum says quietly. For each day of this vacation she has dressed up, curled her hair, carried a good purse. Her milky skin pinkens with adventure, even one this small.

I squint at Mrs. Taylor's picture, looking for terror in that face and finding nothing but a bleak resolve. She's consigned to something she can't undo; the only way forward is over that booming falls. Mum examines each photograph—they're six feet high—her head nodding slowly. The last photo shows Mrs. Taylor being helped out of the barrel at the end of her tumble, hair askew but otherwise all buttoned up. I can't stop staring, either, unable to reconcile this mousy old gal with her crazy brand of courage. I observe her at close range, as Mum does, committing her to memory.

"You have to hand it to the woman," Mum says. "She wasn't afraid of *her* shadow."

"Come on, Margaret," Father Bob says. "Let's get this train moving."

At the wax museum Mum lingers again, this time over the new installment, the big draw: a likeness of Jackie Kennedy. We ogle the display as if we've just run into a relative we forgot we had. Arms crossed, Mum eyes the creepy wax figure top to bottom, pillbox hat to spunky black pumps.

"What do you think, Mum?" we ask. She's the Jackie expert.

She takes another moment, considering the boxy suit, the wedding ring, the fake pageboy hair. "Quite realistic," she says, nodding. "Very good."

Of course we agree.

A week after leaving our tensed-up town, we cruise back into Mexico at midafternoon, we girls wearing new T-shirts and carrying *Maid of the Mist* change purses we plan to distribute to our friends.

Anne notices first. I hear a little intake of breath. "What—?"

A band of men, each carrying a big sign, heads across the footbridge.

"Sweet Mother of Mary," Mum says. "We're on strike."

14

∼

I Hear Music

THE *Times:* STRIKE ENTERS SECOND WEEK.

In school—sixth grade under way—I spend long fuddling afternoons learning equations from Sister Yvonne-Marie, a doe-eyed giant who loves math. My classmates are having trouble sitting still. As our hills redden, some of the fathers have left town to work the apple harvest, others to make long, dismal drives to investigate other mills in new towns, new states, some as far away as New Jersey. My brother, having hired a booking agent for the Impacts, is singing all over New England between gigs at the Rumford AmVets. Management—this is how we refer to Bill Chisholm and his cohort now—has dug in for the long haul, and so has the union, and now that the fathers are leaving town in search of work, the tensions have trickled all the way down to children at their desks trying to solve for x.

I observe my classmates in wonder and amazement:

Their fathers are gone. They drum their pencils on their desks. They tap their feet on the bright waxed floor. I feel all grown-up.

To my relief, Mr. Vaillancourt has stayed put. He logs walking shifts at the lower gate with other strikers who hold up signs and sing "Solidarity Forever" and pump their fists at the honking traffic. For this the union will pay him twenty-one dollars a week.

On a blustery day that scatters leaves across the strike-calmed surface of the river, Bill Chisholm comes to town from his house in Manhattan to explain his dilemma on WRUM: profits down, competition up, expansion forcing management to get more efficient. That word again. *All for you*, he insists, then asks the strikers to ask themselves: *What will this strike mean to your family?*

What can he be thinking, this third-generation president, as he speaks into the microphone at WRUM? Despite having married the daughter of a foreman from the beater room, Bill lacks his forebears' knack for attracting loyalty. He took office in 1956, a year in which he beat his old man's production by 230,000 tons. Elvis was king and so were we, king of paper, tip tops. Bill thought he'd inherited an American golden age of machine-coated paper, the kind that made magazines shine, a product of Chisholm ingenuity and Chisholm false starts and Chisholm do-overs and massive outlays of Chisholm cash. Hugh the first had built the place up from a raging river and vacant land; Hugh II had gambled on high-gloss and won big; and grandson Bill reinvested the winnings, deploying that Chisholm instinct to build-build-build, against an incoming tide of competition. New steam plant, power station, supercalender, pulp bleachery. The smiling man holding the scissors at one ribbon cutting after another had spoken for years of super-expansion and super-profits, the frosting on the frosting on the cake of our fathers' lives.

Now he sits in an overheated Rumford radio station, sliding those heavy glasses up on his nose, addressing a nervous, angry populace whom he's come to think of as family. But the days of complimentary Christmas turkeys are over.

The *Times:* STRIKE ENTERS THIRD WEEK.

Negotiations break down again over crew sizes. In the grip of a late-September stalemate, Bill Chisholm implores us again: *I have returned to talk to you today because of my deep personal interest and affection for Rumford and its surrounding area. . . .* "Surrounding area" means us. His voice slides through the light static, steady and sincere. *May I now refer to some comments that have come to my attention,* he continues, meaning the strikers' vocal yearnings for the "Good Old Days of the Oxford"—which he might rightly interpret as a call for his forebears to return from the dead and save us. *We are all aware that many changes have taken place within the Oxford, particularly over the past three years,* he goes on, referring to the massive cash outlay for build-build-build.

Everything in this speech sounds like job cuts, but before we can reflect on the nuance of rhetoric, he appeals to the sentimental heart of our town, our history, our core identity: *A good many of you people have worked for the company a good many years, and many of your fathers and grandfathers did also—as did mine.* He asks for a gut check: *Down the years, work has been steady for you at the Oxford, and your wage scale and fringe benefits have been very fair.*

At the Vaillancourts' these words are listened to, turned over, wondered about, as Mr. Vaillancourt leaves once again for the gates with his sign.

The *Times:* FEDERAL MEDIATORS ARRIVE AT OXFORD.

The *Times:* 200 SALARIED WORKERS LAID OFF; CHIS-HOLM TO ANNOUNCE SALARY CUTS.

Mum says, "You stay here tonight. That poor woman has enough mouths to feed. Besides, I want you here. I want you girls here."

I gaze across to the Vaillancourts' block, the school beyond, the mill looming over it all. I breathe in, but the smell is gone. The smell of bread and butter, Dad always said. The smell of money.

What will this strike mean to your family?

The *Times:* STRIKE ENTERS FIFTH WEEK.

"What will this strike mean to our family?" I ask Mum, as she sets out the real bread and butter we have in abundance thanks to FDR. "What, Mum? What will this strike mean to our family?"

The inconceivable answer: Nothing.

Strike or no strike, we can still live here because we can live anywhere. But we don't want to live anywhere. We want to live here, in Mexico—our Mexico, the only one we know.

I lie awake for nights thereafter, imagining a town in which we are the only residents—the five of us and a handful of others who stayed: old Mr. Arsenault with his hound dog; the Norkuses scowling at the emptied sky; a few nuns waiting to be reassigned; another fatherless family or two, living on Social Security. I imagine Denise's family leaving town forever in Mr. Vaillancourt's Plymouth, off to a New Jersey mill or one in Minnesota, where they'll have to make friends with people who have never heard of Moxie.

What will this strike mean to your family?

The real answer: Everything. Without the mill there's no work and without work there's no money and without money there's no Nery's, no Bowl-O-Drome, no Larry's, no Fisher's, no Chicken Coop, no Doris's Dress Shop, no Lamey's, no Lazarou's Motor Sales. Without the mill, one by one the neighbors will leave, one by one the schools and parishes will close, one by one the thriving little businesses where the clerks know us by name will board up their windows and lock up their doors.

Perhaps others—other kids, other grownups—lie awake with these same fears, for after six and a half tense, troubling weeks, the news travels like light from the lower gates to the riverfront to Main Street, from house to house to house.

Our phone rings. "I just heard," Mum says to Barry. "Thank God." That's what everybody says: *Thank God thank God thank God.* The steam-plant workers report back first, on the Sunday-night third shift. Pulping operations resume on Monday-morning first shift, and from there it takes thirty-six more hours to feed the pulp through all the systems, producing the first post-strike roll of paper.

At the Vaillancourts I discover that my place at the table has not, as I feared, been snatched up by someone else. There it is, just as I left it. Mr. Vaillancourt can't contain his relief, eyeing his laden table like a man presiding over a banquet, doling out second helpings for everyone.

Unbeknownst to him, I've been writing a new book—with full-page illustrations done in crayon and colored pencil—called *Omer and Brownie: A Love Story.* When I present it to him after supper, quaking with adoration, he blushes and says, *Isn't this something* and laughs that chuckling laugh as I nearly implode with pleasure. Forty-five years later, Mrs. Vaillancourt—Theresa—will unveil *Omer and Brownie,* kept over all those decades, through our growing up and her growing old, and we'll page through it at her kitchen table, which will be downstairs by then, the block bought from the landlords and converted to a single-family, Denise's old room now a repository for objects incandescent with memory, the mill's power and glory ebbing, and Omer twelve years gone.

I'd remembered *Omer and Brownie* as an homage to Mr. and Mrs. Vaillancourt, who were made for each other and called each other "honey" and kissed right in front of us sometimes. I'd remembered a jaunty story about a lady duck who falls in love, despairs when her beloved swims briefly away, then rejoices upon his return. They thought it was about them. I thought it was about them. But really it was about me and Mr. Vaillancourt. And *really* really, it was about me and Dad. Or maybe it was about loss itself—of people, livelihood, love—the things we lose and manage to find again. This is what it is to be twelve, or thirty, or fifty-five: to look back, with new eyes, on what you did not know you knew.

Mmm. Smell that? That's the mill starting up. Everybody takes a deep, grateful breath of it. The counterman at Nery's waits in unaccustomed patience as we choose our nickel's worth of penny candy. *Take your time, girls.* The booths fill up again at Dick's and the Chicken Coop, the new cars at Lazarou's begin to move off the lot, the men who left to pick apples are hurrying home twenty miles over the speed limit. Everyone so relieved, so glad to be working, already forgetting.

We gaze across the river at the big fat clouds and applaud. Sister Yvonne-Marie says, "No homework tonight, boys and girls." Mr. Vaillancourt gets called in—the Number Ten having trouble getting back online. *What competition?* he seems to say as he heads toward the footbridge that leads to Hugh Chisholm's brilliant, opportune, lucrative, fully bloomed idea. *We're the best papermakers in the world.*

It takes three days to restart an idled paper mill, and much more time than that for a twenty-three-year-old school-teacher to finally learn the basics of driving. Norma does the honors, taking Anne out in Dad's "new" car, his sea-green Chrysler Newport, our own riderless horse. It, too, has been unceremoniously idled—for a year and a half now, but after a perfunctory throat-clearing it signals a clarifying, clean-engine all-clear.

The car's a charmer; Anne can see why Dad loved it. Stick shift, four-on-the-floor, smooth-moving, and big in back. Like Black Jack, Dad's Chrysler bucks and stalls down Gleason Street, up Mexico Avenue, and back down Roxbury Road on its maiden voyage, but by week's end its new mis-tress has gotten the hang of shifting and they're off again. With Norma riding shotgun, calmly giving directions, Anne cruises down to Main Street, inviting jokey horror from her students, especially the licensed boys loitering in front of the Bowl-O-Drome, who will swarm her in homeroom the next day and offer to teach her themselves. They call the car "her," the "green dream," and wonder how fast she'll go.

Then comes a day when we wait for the verdict. I'm watching out the kitchen window again, the way I did on the morning Dad died.

"It won't happen any faster with your face glued to the glass," Mum says. She, too, is antsy, pretending to wipe down the stove.

"Hey!" I shout. "She's here! Everybody, hey, she's here!"

Ohhh, my mother sings. *Ohhh*. Cathy and Betty switch off

the Saturday cartoons and jumble out to the kitchen. Now we're all at the window, watching Dad's car round the corner of Worthley Avenue and slide audaciously *into the driveway*.

That's a clue. But we're not sure, until, after a moment of exquisite suspense, we hear the jolly rooty-toot of the horn.

"She got it!" Mum shouts. "She got it!"

"She got it!"

"She got it!"

"SHE GOT IT!"

Norma gets out of the passenger side and waves up at us.

"Come on, girls," Mum says, grabbing a sweater. "Come on!"

We stampede downstairs, past the nodding Norkuses (they approve!), and into Dad's car we go, hooting our congratulations. Anne backs us into the street and takes us for a ride just for the plain joy of riding as we talk over each other — *Was the man nice? Was the test hard? Did he make you park?* — and jounce in our seats and sing the car-trip song and wave out the windows to our friends and neighbors.

The strike is over and we're living again among three thousand fully employed papermakers and fourteen thousand citizens across our two towns, ten thousand in Rumford, four thousand in Mexico. We are part of this prosperous, invincible place.

From this shimmering perch, who can imagine the strike of '64 as the last civilized walkout, the last conflict of the "Good Old Days of the Oxford"? Who here can imagine the strikes of our future: hired replacements we'll call "scabs"; families permanently scorched by betrayal; ultimatums written in spray paint and buckshot; the union's broken back; the mill's changing names?

The strike has tolled the first, faint alarm for what is to come, a slow vanishing, almost imperceptible at first, another thousand souls gone away at the threshold of each coming decade, a slow, unstoppable dwindling that will carry through the next ten, twenty, thirty years, until the glorious might of the mighty, mighty Oxford—aka Ethyl, aka Boise-Cascade, aka Mead, aka Mead-Westvaco, aka NewPage—will survive mostly through memory.

But on the morning of Anne's new license we know nothing of this. The strike is done, the father has come back, all is forgiven, the mill breathing hard again on the riverbank.

Anne toots to this one, to that one. On Brown Street we spot Denise waving with both arms. Stop the car! Hop in! *I hear music but there's nooo one there! I smell blossoms but the treees are bare!* Dad's fancy-gorgeous car still smells weakly of Camels. Adults on the street—neighbors, nuns—pause to smile at us, a back-seat jumble of kids no longer exactly children: a sixth-grader, her sixth-grader friend, a fourth-grader, and Betty, a gradeless, eternal child who will stay here forever, though not with her mother—who will die young—but with her big sister, this lovely young teacher at the wheel.

We wave to other kids' mothers, other kids' fathers; we yell out the windows, *Hey, everybody, lookit lookit, she got it!* The grownups nod indulgently. So cute! So lively! So bright! *All day long I seem to waaalk on air! I wonder whyyy! I wonder whyyy!* They want Mexico's children to be educated, these mothers and fathers and teachers. They want us to know something of the larger world. To live better than they did.

Have they worked out their plan to its inevitable conclusion? Grownups stand at the front of classrooms, they put hamburg steak on supper tables, they sell insurance, they operate heavy machinery, they administer vaccinations, they paint our peeling houses. They cross the footbridge into the Oxford three times a day and come out again, full of their children's dreams. Do they not hear that distant tolling, that low, plangent harmony line in the song they have made of us?

How can they not know? Their children will leave them.

Anne drops Denise at her house. "Come on up," Denise says.

But I don't come on up. I stay here, in this Dad-smelling space. With Mum *ooh*ing and *aah*ing in the front, with Anne providing such an even, reassuring ride, with all of us together in this car Dad once drove, I prefer at last to come home. *Stars that used to twinkle innn the skies! Are twinkling innn my eyes! I wonder whyyy!* Anne rounds the block and eases Dad's car to a soft, complete, textbook stop at 16 Worthley Avenue. In the driveway. *Good job, Annie! Yaaay!*

I breathe in a feeling—a feeling I've heard tell of: everything falling into place. Until now, I didn't know what *everything* meant. Or *place*.

Everything means us.

Place means us.

This feeling is *us* falling into *us*.

And *us* is this family of women, singing the car-trip song. There is no journey we cannot make this way.

Epilogue: NewPage

I N ONE OF MY last vivid memories of my mother standing, she lingers at the parlor door in her housedress and white Mary Janes, digging her toe into the rug, a nervous habit. Denise and I are running lines for our Mexico High School junior-class production of *Our Town*, directed by Miss Anne Wood, our English teacher. There's Mum, a damp dishtowel held at her hip, her head at a bird-cocked angle, toe twisting slowly, something on her mind. She has just lost her younger sister, our aunt Sadie, a small, dimpled fifty-year-old whose husband had whisked her off to New York State and kept her there, until she came back home to die. Another sweet shriveling person in a cancer bed.

Maybe Sadie's on her mind as she watches us rehearse. Denise, playing Rebecca, has been typecast as the little sister, the big-blue-eyed innocent. I've got the role of Emily, the small-town girl who dies in childbirth in Act Three, comes back as a spirit, and discovers the ignorance of the living. "I didn't realize," the dead, distraught Emily says to the wise old Stage Manager. "So all that was going on, and we never noticed." He'd warned her not to go back, not to visit the living in any form, but would she listen? No. And now her unchecked impulse has revealed to her how blind she was to life's daily wonders. The stage directions call for sobbing, which I can't manage on cue.

Mum drops the towel over a chair back and offers to interpret my lines. "You don't sound sad enough," she tells me. "Let me try." Flabbergasted, I give up my copy of the script. My mother, who as far as I know has never stood on a stage — has never even been to a real play — is about to give me acting lessons. I'm sixteen years old in this memory. I already know everything.

She clears her throat and makes an entrance, a step and a half to the center of the room. Flicking us a glance I can't interpret, she runs her finger down the page, folds back the spine, then clears her throat again, a self-conscious little scratch.

"I didn't realize," she begins, reciting the way she sings, pulling syllables like taffy, making you think about the person who wrote the words. She declaims Emily's entire goodbye-world speech, her voice rolling and dropping like a storm-tossed Irish sea. "Goodbye to clocks ticking," she laments. "And Mama's sunflowers. And food and coffee. And new-ironed dresses, and hot baths. And sleeping and waking up. Oh, earth, you're too wonderful for anybody to realize you." She looks beyond us to the homely wallpaper she put up, then couldn't afford to replace: monstrous palm fronds floating on a sea-green background. Her eyes shiny and alive, she searches out her invisible audience behind the foliage, and I can almost hear applause.

Her cancer is already forming, unbeknownst. I see her in silhouette—we're at midwinter, the sun setting too early, and behind her, through the parted curtains on the parlor window, I can make out the coughing smokestacks of the Oxford. Only we're not the Oxford anymore in this year of *Our Town*. Bill Chisholm and a group of men sold us to a chemical company that goes by the ugly name of Ethyl. We are the "Oxford segment of the Ethyl Corporation."

We are the segment. The mighty, mighty segment.

At the long-service banquet just after the sale, Bill Chisholm repeated the oft-told history of the Oxford and added Ethyl as the latest gleaming chapter in the book of us. *I see no change anywhere*, he assured the gathered workers, who were hushed, wary, a little too warm in their banquet clothes. The Ethyl CEO then got up and proclaimed the horrifying sale *the best kind of merger that can take place in American business*. After that, everyone dug in to a roast-beef dinner and a musical entertainment by a "fine young tenor" currently burning up the New England music circuit. He sang like an archangel, and when he finished everybody stood up for the local son, now living in Portland and really going places, this boy who had found my father.

"Do any human beings ever realize life while they live it?" Mum, as Emily, goes on. "Every, every minute?"

We wait. She waits. Then Denise checks her script and reads the Stage Manager's famous reply: "No," she says, following the line with her finger. "The saints and poets, maybe. They do some."

Mum nods. Closes her eyes. Says, "I'm ready to go back."

I watch this spectacle in a state of wonder and melancholy. A life flashes before my eyes. Not mine; hers. Or an unlived version of hers, one where she offers herself to a world beyond us. Saying these lines with such sympathy and conviction, she is neither my shy, my sad, my only mother with her unfinishable loss, nor the woman she might be if Dad were still here, but somebody else altogether, an imaginative stranger with an inner life just like mine, aching with secret hopes for her own marvelousness. I feel my own self exposed, my own rickety purchase on my own fleeting life uncovered as my mother stands before me in the winter light, reading the lines of a mourning girl.

She hands back my script and waits modestly. "That was great, Mrs. Wood," says Denise. She means it. My dear friend.

"That *was* great," I tell her. I feel, strangely, like crying. "Really, Mum. Thanks."

"Try it again," she urges me. Behind her, through the window, above the river, an Ethyl steam cloud wisps into the reddening sky. In Grovers Corners, the town in the play, nothing will ever change. In our town, where a decade is ending, the Oxford signs, which stood for nearly seventy years, have been switched to Ethyl long enough now to look normal; the shoe industry has all but expired; and Anne has lost her first student to Vietnam.

I snatch up the scripts and put them in my book bag. "Later, maybe. We've got other homework."

"I'll sit right here," Mum insists. "I'll be the audience."

But I say no; those half-memorized lines have hit me blind-side and I can't bear to visit them just now. When the curtain finally goes up in the Mexico High School auditorium, Mum applauds my portrayal of Emily, whose fictional losses so embrace me on opening night that the tears I pretend to cry in Act Three turn to real tears dripping off my chin. Mum watches from the second row — wearing pretty shoes made someplace else, holding a program printed on Ethyl paper.

What does it mean to love a place? This town, with its steam-pumping heart, loved the people who first loved me. As I return here now, passing the WELCOME TO MEXICO sign, I see up ahead my father's ghost on the footbridge, his dusty boots, his cap and pail. I swing by the Norkus block, slow down, look up, and there's my mother shimmering on the screen porch, lifting the bird to her lips, confiding a word into his invisible ear. The stairs once patrolled by the long-gone Norkuses want paint; the garden's an overgrown thicket, the driveway a frost-heaved mess after another heartless winter.

On Main Street, Dick's is still here, and the Chicken Coop, but the car dealerships are gone, and the dress shops, and the roller rink. The Bowl-O-Drome is now a vacant lot, its embankment leading up to the empty convent, the defunct church, the closed school. All around me, signs of wear. Perhaps my hometown always looked this way, and my recall has been shaded by a desire to shine up the past.

By the time my mother died, three years after her catastrophic cancer surgery, my sisters and I had learned to interpret the garbled language of her stroke; how to gentle her paralyzed arm through the sleeve of a brand-new blouse; how to change a bed with our vanishing mother still in it; how to surrender to the art of "offering it up." Despite the despair that floated in and out like an Oxford steam cloud, we learned also to find the blessing in the disguise of Dad's death—his death, after all, had prepared us for hers—because we loved our mother and believed what she'd always said: "God provides, girls. We don't always see it until after."

We'd had to move three blocks from 16 Worthley Avenue, to a ground-floor rent to accommodate the clanking bulk of Mum's wheelchair. On moving day we carried our things down the three flights. We carried the jewelry box. The turkey pan. The kitchen chairs and the birdcage. The adding machine. The toy piano. The pictures of Pope John and President John and the Sacred Heart of Jesus. The things we carried had made the Norkus block our home, the only one we'd ever known.

Father Bob couldn't lift much weight. Mr. Vaillancourt managed the heavy stuff—the beds, the dressers, the red couch. Turns out we didn't have much in the way of bulk. Mostly, we carried little things. The electric fry pan. A box of Anne's peep-toe shoes. Three eight-pound cats. Trip after trip, down the stairs and up, too much stairs now for sure.

Our mother died in the new apartment, on a December evening in her freshly made bed, while we girls chatted quietly in the kitchen, making supper. She died having been cared for by the children she'd taught, through her own example, how to bear up, be brave, look for blessings in disguise. The first person at our door the next morning was Mrs. Vaillancourt, holding a tray of biscuits. At the wake we saw our longtime neighbors, the Fleurys and the Gallants and the Gagnons and the O'Neills; we saw men from the mill; we saw priests and monsignors of Father Bob's acquaintance, six of whom would concelebrate the funeral; we saw the whole of our town, it seemed—the town that could not be separated from our mother or father or us, not now or ever.

And finally, at the bitter end of that wintry evening, we saw—inching down the carpeted aisle toward Mum's glossy casket—the Norkuses. It had been three years. They were older than I'd ever realized, nearly to their nineties, leaning on each other in a way that rekindled my image of the young immigrants arriving with rags on their feet.

"Respect to Missus," they said. "Too much sad."

Too much sad. Father Bob succumbed a decade after that, also of cancer. After his diagnosis he retired from duty and spent the happiest year of his life, back in the town where he was born, in the company of Anne and Betty, living the humdrum domestic life he'd always wanted in a house filled with the sound of women.

It's not our past I wish to conjure today, however; it's our future. I've driven here, from my house in Portland, to help Anne plan her wedding. Her first wedding, to her first true love. She is sixty-eight years old but still resembles the sweet young teacher who inhabits this book. Anne's groom—her equal in vivacity and compassion—is the director of Hope Association, a sheltered workshop for adults like Betty, who's been a day client there for thirty-five years, making rolling pins, toy blocks, and lifelong friends.

Cathy, too, is on her way to town, driving up from Massachusetts, where she's a vice president of a Catholic college, work she loves. She's still the take-charge girl: We have flowers to pick out, menus to plan, a program to nail down, and these things cannot be done without her.

Anne always loved Jane Austen, who liked to end her books with a wedding. Imagine my delight, to end my book with this one. After a lifetime of caring for us, for Betty, for her students, for everybody else, our Anne has fallen for a man who wants to care for her.

Cathy's husband will walk Betty to her seat of honor. My husband—my Rumford boy—will play the processional on guitar. Barry, retired from the mill but still gigging, will escort the bride. Cathy and I will sing an old song in a harmony learned long ago from Sister Louise. Denise, who made her career in Our Nation's Capital as a public-health expert at the World Bank, will be sitting with her mother, near the front. After the ceremony, guests from the two towns will celebrate big, for Anne's reach here—the high schools merged years ago—is rich and long.

And after that? Happily ever after, what else? This is what we all believe, because if my family has learned anything from our intermittent sorrows, it is this.

As I drive over the Mexico-Rumford bridge on the way to a house Anne has bought with her groom, the valley opens like a coat I can't wait to put on. The cleaned-up river makes its old ribboning trail. The mill—now, as then—hunkers on the riverbank, outsize witness to my childhood. The Oxford, with its bruising power to give and take, was my first metaphor. I pull over to give it a good look.

I was there, it tells me, still pushing smoke signals into the sky. Beneath those clouds, I experienced the shock of loss, the solace of family, the consolation of friendship, the power of words, the comfort of place. Beneath those clouds, I learned that there is, as my birthday Bible instructed me at age ten, a time for every season. Beneath those clouds, my parents died before their time. But they lived here, too, thankful for their chance.

The sign across the river says NewPage, after the investment company that bought out Mead-Westvaco, which bought out Mead, which bought out Boise-Cascade, which bought out Ethyl, which bought out the Oxford. They've just shut down the Number Ten—temporarily; again—another two hundred jobs gone. The mill looks like an animal that has outlived its ecosystem. Huge, beached, but still breathing. When did it cease to sound like God and instead like an old man wheezing? *Puff . . . puff . . . oooom*, it says, sighing over what might be its last generation of children, most of whom, like me, will make a break for it when they come of age and spend the rest of their lives looking back.

Of course they will. There is such joy here. The day is chilly, the sky so high, the steam clouds shaking with memory.

Thank you, I tell the dying beast. *I forgive you.*

Acknowledgments

Gail Hochman, my brilliant and tireless agent, read multiple drafts of this book and made it so much better every time. Bless you, Gail, for this and everything.

Many thanks to the good people of Houghton Mifflin Harcourt, who embraced me as a new author. Deanne Urmy, my compassionate editor, thank you for your fierce devotion to this book. I'm so glad we've met at last. Much appreciation to copyeditor Barbara Wood, whose excellent work saved me from public disgrace, and to Martha Kennedy and Brian Moore for their thoughtful design. Thanks also to production editor Beth Burleigh Fuller, for making it all work.

Dan Abbott lived this book with me; thank you, sweetheart.

I thank also my angelic sisters—Anne, Catherine, and Elizabeth—for allowing me to write about them so deeply.

And my big brother, Barry, for adding to the final polish, not to mention for all the music over the years.

It takes a village to write a book about a village. I'm indebted to so many people for sharing their knowledge and memories. The librarians at the Rumford Public Library, especially Sharon Madore, had to set me up anew on a balky microfiche every time I came in. The ladies at the Rumford Historical Society—Dru Breton and Myrtle McKenna—offered ongoing good cheer and allowed me to look at original copies of the *Rumford Falls Times* from the 1960s, which helped me immeasurably. The Mexico Historical Society offered me my first chance to speak publicly about my book, which led me to people who once worked with my father. Tiny historical societies like these exist all over America, usually run by volunteers who have taken on the thankless task of preserving the story of us. If your town has one, for God's sake, give them some money.

Many thanks to Mike Madore, for so patiently talking me through the papermaking process; to Harry Carver, for sharing his memories of my father and his work; and to Lucienne (Gagnon) Buckingham, for granting me a poignant afternoon in her kitchen to reminisce about sewing shoes. Norma (Hickey) Berry answered my questions by return e-mail, sent me photographs of the Wood girls as children, and added details to my recollection of our colorful landlords. Thank you to Margie (Lavorgna) Evans for her childhood friendship during a tender time. I owe more to Theresa Vaillancourt than I can ever express, but I thank her here specifically for saving my first completed book, *Omer and Brownie*, all these years. And to Denise Vaillancourt, who cried her way through early drafts, just as I predicted: Denise, your enduring friendship is my treasure.

Wes McNair first urged me to write about my hometown for the anthology *A Place Called Maine*, published by Down East Books. I'm so grateful. My pal Amy MacDonald accompanied me, at a nearby table in the University of New England library, throughout the writing of this book. Hannah Holmes offered tea and sympathy (wine and sympathy, to be precise) at critical junctures. Susan Nevins came up with the title and offered me her camp at Moosehead for the writing of Chapters 4 and 5. Ann Shenassa and Mindy Fleishman, dear old friends, spent a weekend reading the final draft aloud to me. And I owe an unrepayable debt to Polly Bennell, who picked me up at a low, low point and coached me through the beginning, the middle, and the end. Polly, you have no idea.

Last, another nod to my sister Catherine, whose memories can hardly be separated from mine. She made me start all over again, from a first draft that read like an appliance manual. *Ecana egala* forever, Cath.